Chasing
Graveyard
Ghosts

MELBA
GOODWYN

Chasing Graveyard Ghosts

INVESTIGATIONS OF HAUNTED AND HALLOWED GROUND

Llewellyn Publications
Woodbury, Minnesota

First Edition
First Printing, 2011

Based on book design by Steffani Sawyer
Cover art © iStockphoto.com/Jonas Engström
Cover design by Lisa Novak
Editing by Connie Hill

Llewellyn Publications is a registered trademark of Llewellyn Worldwide Ltd.

Library of Congress Cataloging-in-Publication Data

Goodwyn, Melba.
  Chasing graveyard ghosts : investigations of haunted and hallowed
ground / Melba Goodwyn.
      p.   cm.
  Includes bibliographical references.
  ISBN 978-0-7387-2126-2
  1. Haunted cemeteries 2. Ghosts. 3. Sepulchral monuments. 4. Tombs. I. Title.
  BF1474.3.G66   2011
  133.1'22—dc22   2010038824

Llewellyn Publications
A Division of Llewellyn Worldwide Ltd.
2143 Wooddale Drive
Woodbury, MN 55125-2989
www.llewellyn.com

Printed in the United States of America

OTHER BOOKS BY THIS AUTHOR

Ghost Worlds

This book is dedicated to my very dear friend, Sharon Rose McDonald Howe, whose enthusiastic love of ghosts, cemeteries, and paranormal mysteries has enriched my life and broadened my horizon.

CONTENTS

Our Practice is not to clear up the Mystery
It is to make the Mystery clear.
—ROBERT AITKEN ROSHI

ACKNOWLEDGMENTS

My sincerest appreciation goes out to so many people who helped with the creation of this book. I deeply appreciate the assistance of all the genealogists, cemetery personnel, historians, and everyone who has shared information.

I especially want to thank the following individuals for their constant encouragement and for listening to all my ideas and stories (often repeatedly) while I compiled information and researched folklore, urban legends, and secrets of long ago.

First, foremost and always my deepest gratitude goes to my husband, Franklin, and my children: Douglas, Tammy, Dennis, and my twin daughters Peggy Lyn (see, I put your name first) and Patty Jo.

My sincere appreciation goes to Kay Ainsworth, my discerning friend and proofreader who always adds an intuitive ear to whatever I say or write. I wonder if she reads my mind. And to her husband, Chuck, my appreciation for sharing his humor and encouraging words. They always make me happy.

My warmest gratitude goes to Larry and Sharon Howe whose constant supportive friendship has kept me focused on my writing. My special thanks to Sharon, for her constant enthusiasm as we stumbled through the darkness of one haunted cemetery after another looking for ghosts and intriguing mysteries to explore.

Special thanks to my friends and fellow ghost hunters for their encouragement, laughter, and insights into the hidden realm of ghosts and spirits.

INTRODUCTION

My introduction to ghost hunting came through a meeting with Sharon Howe, the founder of TPI (Texarkana Paranormal Investigators). She had placed an ad in our local newspaper for a new ghost hunting group that was forming, offering an open invitation to anyone who was interested in ghosts and paranormal events.

Although I have always been clairvoyant and needed no validation in this area, I was curious about being able to prove the existence of the things that I had been seeing and hearing my entire life.

I was also intrigued by the equipment she brought to the meeting and my enthusiasm for ghost hunting grew rapidly. Of course I attended the first official ghost hunt and was hooked forever. To be able to record, photograph, and document paranormal anomalies was absolutely fascinating to me.

Cemetery investigations were a natural outcome of ghost hunting and before long I was visiting one cemetery after another in search of spirited activity. As I explored the paranormal realm of ghosts, I began to document anomalies and experiences, some of which have helped to shape this book.

Although there have been many books written about cemeteries, ghosts, unique tombstones, unusual epitaphs, and mysterious burials; I have taken a different approach in my investigations of cemetery mysteries. Being clairvoyant gives me the unique advantage of receiving intuitive, clairaudient information as I explore the occult realm of cemeteries and conduct investigations.

I also apply my knowledge of astrology and numerology to the deceased person's birth and death data, names, and even the events surrounding their oftentimes mysterious deaths. This allows me to glean additional information and sometimes incredible insights into their lives. Lastly, I have used my skills as a genealogist to research old records and historical documents to add further clarity and validity to each mystery.

The more I investigated, the more I began to feel like a detective, as each investigation very subtly became a journey into the unknown. I was caught up in the allure of ghosts, urban legends, folklore, and mysterious secrets from long ago.

As a tribute to our loved ones, we traditionally erect monuments and tombstones because we want them to be remembered. In our quest for immortality we leave our personal legacies in marble and granite, inscribed with unusual epitaphs and cryptic messages. Even in death we can still make an impact on those we leave behind, as well as future generations who will read them. In a sense we speak to them from beyond the grave.

I have always found cemeteries to be mysterious worlds, separate, yet intertwined with our own. The ghosts who reside there have always intrigued me and increased my curiosity. I believe we are to accept them as an integral part of our society, whether we choose to acknowledge them or not.

Although cemeteries and graveyards are often filled with mysterious ghosts, and huge overwhelming monuments, they are also filled with beauty, art, and history, and yes, sometimes mysteries to be uncovered and solved.

Some of the mysteries in my book have been solved, but many will remain open and subject to further investigation by those who are as inquisitive as I am. I hope you will enjoy reading about my adventures as I searched through one cemetery after another and uncovered mystery after mystery. Perhaps you will detect or intuit clues that I have missed. If you do, all the better, especially if it intrigues you enough to explore more cemeteries and investigate your own mysteries.

In cemeteries all over the world millions of people have been buried, are being laid to rest today, and will continue to be interred in the future. Each of these people has lived and died and has a story to tell, or perhaps even a mystery to uncover. Each tombstone or monument represents their lives in one way or another.

These are some of their stories...

ONE
HAUNTED OR
HALLOWED GROUND

Every town in America, no matter how small or how large, has a cemetery or graveyard. And almost every graveyard or cemetery has a ghost, and in many cases, several. Every state in the union, every country, every island paradise, and in fact, even the farthest reaches of the earth have designated land that is reserved for the interment of the deceased.

Whether that land is *haunted* or *hallowed* is a different story and the catalyst for this book.

Cemeteries seem to affect most people in very profound ways. Visitors usually experience a wide range of emotions upon entering them. From tearful sadness to reverent silence, they wander among the graves. A ghost hunter or paranormal investigator intent upon the discovery of ghostly activity will no doubt feel anxiety and excited anticipation as he or she explores one cemetery after another.

Cemeteries also evoke thoughts of death and dying, as memories and mysteries, as well as friends, lovers, and ancestors who have transcended our reality for another mysterious realm of spirit are brought together in peaceful repose.

Cemeteries and graveyards are places where most people feel free to express their heartfelt emotions and in doing so create huge reservoirs of psychic energy. They imprint their feelings onto the electromagnetic energy field that surrounds the cemetery, allowing others to sense, see, and even hear their grief and emotions at times.

Nearly everyone acknowledges that these peaceful retreats for the living are the final resting places for their loved ones. But are they? The soul is not the body—it is capable of manifestation in order to be seen, deliver messages, or simply visit loved ones. Many people may feel a sense of dread or uncomfortable emotions as they think about these secluded cities for disembodied souls. Fear of the unknown may surface unexpectedly, leaving them afraid to face the truth of their own mortality. No matter how strong our beliefs are about death and our immortal souls, we are all eventually transformed to a higher vibration and realm of existence. This is a fact of life that will never cease to be. But, how we are remembered, or not, is up to those we leave behind. Cemeteries offer the living an opportunity to show and tell how they want to be remembered. From elaborate tombstones and statuary to enduring epitaphs we can personally say our final goodbyes forever.

Cemeteries and graveyards are usually considered sacred places, *hallowed* ground regardless of one's religious upbringing or lack of religious beliefs. There are as many different types of burial places as there are diverse cultures and religions.

Usually religions dictate where most cemeteries and graveyards are situated, but wars, fraternal organizations, families, and governments sometimes create and define final resting places for the dead.

Although not less important, but certainly considered by many as less important, some graveyards and burial grounds such as potters fields, or those established out of necessity by sanatoriums, asylums, and prisons are often left abandoned and ignored.

Graveyards and potters fields are also found in most towns and cities across the country. The diversity of the American people is often reflected in their cemeteries. Benjamin Franklin said, "Show me your cemeteries and graveyards and I will tell you what kind of people you have." He obviously used his innate spiritual discernment regarding society as he knew it.

Still others came into existence because the deceased was believed to be too vile or sacrilegious to be buried with the pious people of the towns and communities where they lived. Murderers, witches, adulterers, bastards, strangers, suicides, and all manner of perverse souls were buried in unholy ground that more often than not became "*haunted*" ground due to the lack of spiritual attendance or respect for the human soul.

Land has also been set aside in some towns for beloved pets. Animal cemeteries and burial places are some of the most heartwarming and yet bizarre places I have ever come across. These will be discussed in an upcoming chapter.

While there are many similarities in cemeteries, there are also distinct differences, mostly created by culture and geographical terrain. Although they may be found in the same geographical area, there are always unique aspects that set them apart. For example there is a difference between southern and northern cemeteries, as well as above and below sea-level cemeteries. From the east coast to the west coast cemeteries are established only to later disappear as towns become ghost towns or cities grow up around them and in some cases actually over them.

Whether *haunted* or *hallowed* ground, one thing is for sure; how we are memorialized depends on our loved ones and society as a whole. City cemeteries and rural graveyards are as big a part of our daily lives as the businesses and communities we pass everyday as we go about our daily routines of going to work, school, or simply as we run errands. So why do we look the other way when they come into view? Could it be so the dead don't see us?

There is something very mysterious about distinctive older cemeteries. From the antiquated tombstones and statuary to the eerie mausoleums there are history, art, and perhaps even ghosts waiting for unsuspecting mourners. Whether or not we choose to believe in ghosts, graveyards and ghosts will always be connected in mystifying ways.

Cemeteries are great repositories of history. From the pioneer families who settled our country and the heroes who fought courageously for our freedom to the immigrants who enhanced our societies and even the wayward strangers who added mystique to our existence, cemeteries are keepers of memories and secrets.

If you are into genealogy, you may have discovered that the ghosts of your ancestors encourage you to look for connecting links to families in graveyards and cemeteries both here and abroad. I personally believe we are guided and directed to the gravesites of our ancestors to seek closure, information, and possibly to expose well kept and deeply buried secrets from the past.

We often assume that our cemeteries and graveyards are but hushed reflections of the souls who reside there, when in fact they are much more. Although we live in a death-denying society, the deaths of our loved ones impact our lives daily. Death should be an intimate celebration of everyday life as family and friends all take part in respectful farewells.

Whether it is to say goodbye or to comfort those left behind, it is seldom a solitary undertaking. Flowers, cards, and food are furnished to nourish the bodies and souls of the grieving.

The departed's final resting place may be visited and perhaps re-visited for years to maintain loving contacts, especially in times of emotional turmoil or great sadness. In this sense cemeteries and graveyards have become places where the living can establish links to the past, talk to their loved ones who have transcended death, and ultimately face the truth of their realities.

In the very early days of America's colonization, burial places were often well disguised or completely hidden to keep wild animals from finding them. This resulted in a multitude of unmarked gravesites which are lost to us forever because the tradition of handing down oral information has faded with time, leaving only ghosts to attend those unmarked or undisclosed graves.

During the Puritan era the general focus concerning death was on the destination of the soul. Our forefathers established the churchyard as a place for the burial of prominent Christian townsfolk while the less wealthy and those of lesser importance were buried in graveyards located near, yet still outside the realm of opulence. Although close by or near the edge of town, they were worlds apart in landscape, statuary, and tombstones, and of course, in reverent perpetual care.

Family plots and private burial places were often necessary when rural or plantation living made it impractical to transport the deceased long distances to the nearest town. In the country, private family gravesites were often situated on hilltops or in rocky ground that was deemed unfit for cultivation. Small family plots were created and cared for by family members and friends. These often isolated plots of land not only contained the graves of the landowner's family, but was often shared with friends and neighbors in their time of need.

In the eighteenth century, the focus was not on the dead so much as on those who were left behind. As towns and communities grew, the local churchyards ran out of space, creating a need for the development of new cemeteries on the outskirts of town. A few acres of land were usually purchased or donated by a prominent citizen. This paved the way for a new type of cemetery.

Plain ordinary churchyard burial grounds gave way to the beautiful park-like settings of the Victorian Era. These were usually located some distance from the church, and reflected a distinct atmosphere. As society evolved, many of these lavish cemeteries had spacious landscapes, with stone pathways bordering ponds and huge shade trees. There were also beautiful ornate benches provided for those seeking peaceful reflection. People came to these cemeteries to relax. Friends and lovers could stroll hand in hand as they shared intimate memories or perhaps feelings of love and devotion.

During the late 1800s and early 1900s these lavish cemeteries offered a place for social gatherings that were held with great enthusiasm, as well as picnics that were enjoyed within an atmosphere of serenity and solitude. The reality of death was gently represented by beautiful celestial angels, regal monuments, and engraved epitaphs that were comforting, inspirational, humorous, and sometimes just plain weird.

Today we have a lot of public cemeteries that are owned and maintained by the cities in which they exist. Many of them are ignored unless they are deemed valuable because of historical or picturesque significance. There are also magnificent parks with acres of smooth grassy lawns. The elaborate style of yesterday's tombstones has been replaced by flat markers that lie flush with the ground, primarily for the convenience of the caretakers and mowers.

However, to me these level markers do nothing to capture the essence of the person who is buried there. It's hard to sense the soul in such sterile surroundings.

TWO
GHOST HUNTING IN CEMETERIES

The mixture of belief and disbelief surrounding ghosts only adds to their mystique. Few people can deny that they are fascinated with the idea of apparitions, and disembodied entities. Although they may be frightened most agree that ghosts and mysterious anomalies are indeed worthy of investigation and serious examination.

The basis of a ghost's existence is, of course, energy. They must have energy to manifest, communicate, and move from place to place. When ghosts are active, their energy causes disruptions in the electromagnetic fields around them which are detectable with ghost hunting equipment such as: EMF detectors, EVP recorders, and even dowsing rods.

Whether one believes in ghosts or not, the fact remains that they are mysterious visitors in our cemeteries. There is a lot of controversy about what ghosts are and why they manifest in cemeteries. This usually leads to even more questions. Who are they? When did they die? What do they want? And why did I see them? Why me?

Although people fear being haunted by a ghost, they are just as intrigued by all the controversy that surrounds them. This combination of fear and interest applies to cemeteries as well. Even though ghosts are encountered almost everywhere, I have chosen only to discuss those that appear in cemeteries and graveyards and are seen and heard by unsuspecting mourners, visitors, genealogists, and of course ghost hunters.

Cemeteries, like people, have a past. They have stories to tell and secrets to uncover. What better way to expose those secrets and stories than through paranormal investigations conducted by parapsychologists and ghost hunters who have the utmost respect for the deceased and their places of rest?

However, no matter how convincing the evidence is, there will always be someone, some skeptic, who will try to debunk our findings. Nevertheless, for someone who has had a paranormal experience or an encounter with a ghost, no amount of skepticism will ever change their perception of ghosts and paranormal phenomena.

A CHILDHOOD GHOST STORY

My own fascination with cemeteries and ghosts began when I was only twelve years old. Younger generations, city dwellers, and those not raised in the south may not know about grave-yard workings, but it was an integral part of my childhood summers. Each and every summer on a specific day, family members and friends would gather at our local cemetery for a day of cleaning the graves and sprucing up the graveyard.

My story began when I was a young teenager. I had become bored with going to graveyard workings over the years and now that I was older I thought I should be able to decide whether or not I wanted to go. Other than seeing my cousins, I really didn't have an interest at all in going; well almost no interest—I still wanted one of my grandmother's fried peach pies. I had seen the gathering grow in numbers over the years, and watched relatives come and go, some permanently.

Well, I didn't win the argument with my parents so I went along reluctantly. To be honest, I prayed all night for rain. No luck. However, it was a gloomy, cloudy day that matched my mood rather well. Whether it was the atmospheric changes that day or my somber mood that caused it, I was witness to a ghostly sight, one I will always remember.

I wandered aimlessly around the graveyard, weaving in and out of the old weathered tombstones, determined not to be happy or enthusiastic about the gathering. As I approached the back of the cemetery, my reverie was broken by a wailing sound. Thinking that perhaps a small animal must be hurt I headed off in the direction of the pitiful sound. As I rounded a huge magnolia tree I saw the source of the crying. A young woman was kneeling down beside a cradle that held a sleeping baby. Both were semi-transparent with varying degrees of thickness. I stood there in silent reverence as I witnessed her sorrow. Although I wasn't scared, I was suddenly very cold, and trembling all over. Suddenly they just evaporated before my very eyes. I blinked several times, hoping that I could bring them back, but I couldn't.

My perception of cemeteries was forever changed that day. It was not just a place filled with weird tombstones. It was a place of life and death, and yes, even ghosts. I returned to the gathering in meek acceptance of the reality of ghosts and my own place in their realm of existence. I realized that we share the same space. What a profound insight!

Before we had left home my father had tried to encourage me to go by suggesting that I do some family research while I was there. Some of our ancestors who are buried there pre-dated the Civil War. He tried to instill in me an appreciation of my ancestors as well as cemeteries, but he failed to mention the ghosts who reside there.

After seeing the ghosts, I wanted to know everything about the cemetery, and the people who were buried there. I began my research with the graves where I had seen the mother and baby. I learned that the cemetery was established in the mid-1800s and that its original name was "Dark Corners." Why would anyone name a cemetery Dark Corners? My inquisitive mind coupled with my desire to understand things led me down a fascinating path to uncover this, my first mystery. Although I was prepared to learn perhaps a sinister motive for naming the cemetery Dark Corners, I was surprised to find something altogether different. Evidently, the entire state of Texas was called the "Dark Corners" of the Confederacy during the Civil War. This was because so few battles actually took place within the borders of Texas. I can only surmise that a very patriotic Confederate soldier named this particular cemetery and perhaps the community that once existed nearby.

Cemeteries are open-air repositories of all kinds of energies. Ghosts are not the only entities dwelling there. There are undoubtedly other beings that may be waiting for an opportune time to scare or stalk unsuspecting ghost hunters. Because of this, ghost hunting can be dangerously risky.

Along with these risks, we also face the possibility of meeting our greatest fears, as well as hidden aspects of ourselves. The following story is a good example of how ghost hunters are introduced to new realms of existence where the unseen or hidden suddenly becomes a reality.

VAMPIRE GRAVESITE

"The bat that flies at close of eve,
He's left the brain that won't believe".

—WILLIAM BLAKE

Vampirism is enjoying a resurgence and new popularity today as metaphysical books, television, and the newly emerging gothic subculture appears on the scene. Parents are startled. School officials would rather look the other way, and society as a whole wishes they would just go away. However, vampires and tales of vampirism have been around since recorded history. I seriously doubt that they will simply disappear.

Maybe a good idea would be to try to understand the psychological and paranormal aspects of this supposed dark entity. Do our fears of the unknown allow them to roam the earth in shrouded darkness? Perhaps we would have to face our own inadequacies and obsessions in order to understand this prince of darkness; a scary thought for many people.

Although vampires sleep during the day and live in the dark recesses of the mind at night, they remain shrouded in secrecy. No matter how they choose to reveal themselves to society, one thing is for sure: like ghosts, they reside alarmingly close to the humans they interact with. Vampires are a law unto themselves and as such they are just more alive than they should be or perhaps even desire to be. Unlike ghosts who are more aligned with spiritual evolvement and eternal rest, vampires prefer to blend in with the societies they inhabit in search of immortality.

Because of the ghost stories I had heard and the tales of a vampire grave, I grew up visiting a local graveyard time after time over the years. The ghost lore surrounding this isolated graveyard coupled with stories of the *vampire grave* makes this particular graveyard one of the most intriguing, haunted places I have ever investigated.

Of course, I know that folklore creates its own history and it is often inaccurate. However, that doesn't negate the fact that something strange or paranormal must have taken place in order to create the stories and legends of ghosts and vampires.

Cedar Grove Cemetery is located in a very isolated abandoned community in the southwestern part of Bowie County, Texas. It is overgrown and unattended. The road leading up to it is rough and deeply rutted. Definitely a road less traveled. Enormous oak trees help to keep the graveyard secluded, thereby preserving its mysterious presence.

The lively town of Dalby Springs that once existed nearby now has only one church and a community water well to mark its existence. All the buildings are gone. The town began in 1839 and grew to become a bustling railroad stop. It had a college, a racetrack, five cotton gins, stores and shops, and boasted seven healing springs. Native American tribes used these springs as far back as thirty thousand years ago, evidenced by arrowheads and projectile points, axes, scrapers, and pottery found in the area. These springs came to be known for their unique medicinal value. The curative springs drew large crowds of people from all over the world. The town was the central attraction of the county and the railroad delivered more excitement every day. The magnificent hotel was a hub of activity.

The need for burial space increased as more and more people settled in the area. Visitors increased, many who were seriously ill, as they came to take the cures the spring waters offered. In time the Methodist churchyard could no longer hold everyone, so an additional graveyard was established. It began as a final resting place for the unknown, less fortunate, or criminal element that drifted into town. It was situated away from town and deep in the woods. A church once stood next to the graveyard, but it mysteriously burned to the ground in the early 1900s.

Today the graveyard is scattered with weathered tombstones, many of which are unreadable. Some are broken and lie half-buried among the deep foliage and uneven landscape, while others have been placed up against trees for preservation.

To enter the graveyard, you must first pass through an old iron gate. As you pass through this portal the air feels different. Almost everyone I know has felt a tingling sensation as soon as they enter the gated enclosure. Upon entering the graveyard their emotions change rapidly as if prompted by an unseen force. People hear voices and unusual noises, footsteps crunch the leaves around them, and light anomalies appear and disappear. All of this before even stepping foot inside the graveyard.

The first thing everyone notices is an elaborate six-foot tall fence surrounding a mysterious six- by eight-foot plot. This mysterious gravesite is the rumored burial place of a family of vampires. Until just a few short years ago there was a huge iron spike embedded deep in the middle of the gravesite. It protruded out of the ground as a terrifying testament to what lay beneath. Locals say that there were also two tall flame holders situated at the back corners of the gravesite farthest from the enclosure's locked gate. It was rumored that for years these would burn on certain nights all night long. Who kept them going and why has been lost to history, perhaps never again to shine the light of knowledge on the mysterious vampire grave.

There have been rumors and stories from older locals who say that mysterious Masonic rituals were held in the *"cage."* This particular cemetery is located on the 33rd degree parallel, so undoubtedly it could have had great Masonic value, if it were indeed used for some of their rituals. I am equally intrigued by this information and maybe my continued research will reveal even more bizarre mysteries surrounding this unusual gated plot.

Vandals broke into the plot several years ago and took the flame holders, as well as the gate and the spike that secured the gravesite. I wonder where the vandals are today, or *if* they are?

It's scary indeed to see this gravesite late at night as moonlit shadows move about. One is strangely affected by the presence of this large gated plot set at the back of the graveyard away from the other tombstones. An interesting fact about this grave is that it is obvious that the deceased—if they are indeed deceased—are buried on a north-south line, as opposed to the Christian tradition of burying people on an east-west line.

This indicates that whoever is buried there was considered unworthy of a decent burial. Yet, how does one explain the beautiful iron fence, its unusual height, the two flame holders, the spike, and the gate that stayed locked for well over 150 years and possibly longer? There is no marker and my research reveals that there never has been, only a story passed down from generation to generation with all its sinister and mysterious secrets.

As more and more people in that area die or move away, others seem even more reluctant to tell their stories or talk about the gravesite. Although no one has ever called the rumor a hoax, and many locals are in agreement that a vampire is buried there, they still don't want to talk about it.

However, there is always more than one way to get information. *Enter the ghost hunters!* Motivated by a recent EVP (electronic voice phenomena) recorded by an amateur ghost hunter, we gathered our equipment and mustered our courage on a night of a full moon, and set out to investigate the mysterious vampire grave.

On the tape three people are talking as they walk around and discuss the names and dates on the old tombstones. Intermingled with their voices a deep and sinister voice can be heard saying, "Come to the end of the row, where the dead plague the living." It is clear and concise and no effort is needed to understand its meaning. It is without a doubt the spookiest EVP I have ever heard. And guess what is at the end of two rows of tombstones. You guessed it, the vampire's grave.

We began our investigation about 9 p.m. and by midnight we were rapidly on our way, far away from the vampire grave.

At first things were calm and peaceful. However, as the night deepened and the shadows darkened things that appeared normal suddenly turned paranormal. A huge red orb with menacing eyes began to show up on camera screens, footsteps were heard as they crushed the leaves behind us, beside us, and all around us. The atmosphere suddenly became electrically charged, so much so that the hair on the backs of our necks stood up. Scary flapping noises were heard overhead but we couldn't see the source of the noise.

Sharon and I were walking through a very overgrown area beneath a large oak tree when we began to hear a sing-song sound that seemed to fluctuate at different frequencies. We were standing side by side and I could feel the atmosphere around us vibrating. We looked at each other and said at the exact same time, "It's getting louder." Sharon referred to it as a *Sirens Song*, but perhaps it was actually a *Vampire Virtuoso*! Obviously we were being conditioned to hear a message and it came through loud and clear, "Run, heathen, while you still can!"

That little piece of advice was all I needed to get me moving toward the truck. One of younger team members was standing nearby and heard the exchange. He said, "I think I am going to faint!" to which Sharon replied, "If you do we will leave you where you lay." Well, can you believe that he beat us the truck?

I intuitively feel that I have only scratched the surface of what lies beneath the vampire grave. Was the vampire released when the spike was removed and the gravesite desecrated? Does it now reside under cover of darkness in the deeply wooded area surrounding the graveyard? Could this be the reason that over the years more and more people moved and abandoned their homes in the area? Did a family or pack of vampires originally settle in the area because of the health resort? Its constant influx of the sick and infirm could easily have afforded a ready supply of blood for them. So many questions. Now more determined than ever to find the answers, especially after another harrowing experience I had there, which is recorded in my previous book *Ghost Worlds*, I have renewed my quest to find out more about this mysterious cemetery.

Did we actually see a vampire? No. Would we have lived to tell about it if we had? Will we go back to investigate again? Sure.

Ghost hunting in cemeteries and isolated graveyards can be, and sometimes is, very dangerous. Every precaution should be taken to assure everyone's safety. Always visit the cemetery or graveyard for the first time in daylight hours. I can't stress the importance of this aspect of ghost hunting enough. It is absolutely mandatory for the safety of everyone involved. The second-most important thing is to never go alone. To do so is just asking for trouble. You may be walking in almost total darkness or moonlight and probably not paying attention to where you are stepping because you may be distracted by the sights and sounds in the cemetery, not to mention probably looking over your shoulder for ghosts from time to time.

Weather conditions are notorious for creating unsuspected dangers such as uneven terrain and deep crevices caused by wind and water. Graves that have settled and broken headstones may create even more obstacles. Even holes made by gophers and moles can trip up unwary ghost investigators. One could easily break an ankle or leg by stepping into one of these hidden traps. Also beware of embedded tombstones, rocks, fallen limbs, and section markers that may protrude out of the ground. Watch where you are walking. To be honest I have caught my toe on some of these and nearly lost my balance several times. You simply can't see them in the dark.

Cemeteries are not only hosts to ghostly apparitions and paranormal anomalies, but may have other scary natural things as well. There may be poison ivy, spiders, and gigantic gossamer spider webs that reach from tree to tree. We have photographed these beautiful, glistening creations and no doubt many ghost hunters have walked right into them. It makes me shudder just to think about it. No less dangerous are ticks, mosquitoes, and snakes that are hidden beneath leaves, behind tombstones, underneath rocks, and camouflaged in deep foliage. Even a harmless cat can present a scary scenario if it jumps out of a tree and onto the back of an unsuspecting ghost hunter. I have witnessed this and although it was hilariously funny after it was over, it was still a frightening shock for the hunter. Of course, there are actually bats, not to be confused with vampires, and owls whose mournful sounds will make you re-think your investigation entirely.

RONDO CEMETERY

Late one evening TPI members met for our monthly business meeting. Several members expressed a desire to go ghost hunting after the meeting. As we didn't have any calls or leads to follow, we decided to do a cemetery run. Cemeteries are great fun and always a learning experience, especially if we have novice investigators in our group. By the time everyone had gathered we had six carloads of investigators armed with plenty of equipment ready to face the unknown. We set off about 8 p.m. and traveled to cemetery after cemetery. As the night progressed, the size of the group diminished as people tired and went home. Eventually we were down to four members in two cars. Still energized and eager to continue our investigation, we piled into one car and began anew. Yet to visit was a small overgrown, long-forgotten cemetery on the edge of town and a large well-tended cemetery just a few miles outside of town. By now it was 3 a.m. and, as most ghost hunters know, this time of the morning seems to be the witching hour or at the very least, the opportune time to catch ghosts on film.

The first cemetery offered only minor results, a few orbs, some energy streaks, and a faint mist. However, the second cemetery was an entirely different story. Forgetting my own personal motto, always expect the unexpected, I was caught up in the enthusiasm of my friends and failed to pay a lot of attention to my surroundings. With me that morning was Sharon Howe, founder of TPI (Texarkana Paranormal Investigators), Jeremy Crawford, our tech guy, and field investigator Stephen Yarberry. As we drove into the cemetery, we heard an odd screeching sound. I thought for a moment that it might be the car, but as we drove deeper into the cemetery we no longer heard it, so we just assumed it was an owl or something. It was something, all right.

We left the car parked in the middle of the cemetery and started walking in opposite directions of each other. Jeremy and Sharon went one way, while Stephen and I went another. He was walking ahead of me taking video shots with his camcorder, while I lagged behind snapping away with my trusty digital. The cemetery was quiet and serene in the early morning darkness that surrounded us. I was fascinated, as I always am, by the beautiful wrought iron fences enclosing some of the gravesites.

Suddenly, Stephen stopped dead in his tracks. About the same time I noticed two golden orbs in my viewfinder. Wow, I thought, this is cool, and kept walking toward them, taking pictures—totally oblivious to what was really happening. Then I heard Stephen yell, "Oh, shit! Run!"

I caught my breath as he came bounding past me, running backwards at breakneck speed. He was holding his flashlight up in front of him so I could see where I was going. I was amazed at how he was running backwards and missing tombstone after tombstone. His intuition had kicked in and evidently every sense he had was on full alert.

For most women my age, running isn't exactly easy, so I turned to see what had him so upset. At this point, I still wasn't scared, just perplexed. However, when I saw the cause of his concern, I understood all too well. Instead of two amber orbs there were four, and they were attached to two of the blackest, sleekest, panthers I have ever seen out of captivity. Since running was out of the question, I embarked upon a very efficient hustling gait that gained speed as I followed Stephen who was still shining his flashlight forward, while running backwards through clusters of tombstones and monuments.

He yelled for Sharon and Jeremy to get to the car as fast as they could, to let them know that they were in harm's way. As strange as this may sound I started laughing hysterically when I heard Sharon say, "Oh my God, I am going to lose my limbs!"

and then Jeremy's response of "You're going lose more than that if you don't get your ass in gear," really added to my nervous giggling. The whole event actually seemed surreal as we all hit the car at the same time, jumped in, and slammed the doors.

Much to our amazement, just as we were safely seated in the car, the two panthers moved swiftly and silently alongside the car and around in front of it, and then continued their journey toward the edge of the cemetery. Whew! We just sat there speechless for several minutes. Slowly it dawned on us just how lucky we had been. We never expected to run into a pair of panthers in a suburban neighborhood full of houses, churches, and a school.

Our questions came in gasps. Where had they come from? Were they real or surreal? How did they get there? Why didn't they attack us? Not hungry, maybe? Were they forcing us away from something even more sinister at the back of the cemetery? Whatever the case, we were thankful we were able to reach the safety of the car.

We later learned that the panthers had been sighted in that area before and that perhaps their trek through the cemetery was a natural trail they followed. No matter the reason, they woke us up to the fact that you can never be prepared enough, because you never know what you will find. We were looking for ghosts and found quite the opposite.

Most cemeteries have celestial statuary, eerie mausoleums, and ghosts. Of course you can't have all these things without legends, folklore, and rumors sneaking into the mysterious atmosphere of the deceased. There are phenomena about death and cemeteries that we may never understand.

In every country, religion and culture create their own beliefs and customs associated with death and disembodied spirits. Of course, ghost-lore and superstitions are the inevitable outcome of these mysterious phenomena. While some stories may seem utterly ridiculous, others often make us stop and think or at the very least make us more cautious, because as ghost-hunters we really never know what might happen late at night in a darkened graveyard.

Generally the words ghost-lore and superstition carry the negative connotation of ignorance and are often associated with unscientific and uneducated people who live in isolated rural areas. However, this is not the case as everyone has some odd beliefs or an inherent superstition about what causes good luck, bad luck, and what, if anything, provides them with protection. Most people also have fears and beliefs about cemeteries and how we interact with ghosts and spirits.

Perhaps one of the oldest events regarding ghosts and superstitions come from the ghost-lore regarding crossroads. In earlier times murderers, witches, and people who committed suicide were buried at crossroads in a foolish attempt to keep them from returning to the realm of the living. People were often hanged at a crossroads and then buried in secluded areas to keep their spirits from finding their way back to the community.

Another interesting aspect of ghost-lore is the "Grave-Sleeper." Our team has often discussed this and of course we are curious, but not curious enough to try it, yet. Celtic people, especially the Welsh, had a strange ritual to make contact with their ancestors known as grave-sleeping.

Men and women believed to be receptive to the spirit world would sleep on the graves of other's ancestors. If their spirit had messages to convey to family members they would enter the body of the grave sleeper and communicate through them while they were asleep or in a trance state. The "sleeper" would then relate messages from the other side for family and friends. This was a well-known custom and seemed to work well, especially if the ritual took place in a spirit-infested cemetery or graveyard.

It's true that I am clairvoyant, as well as clairaudient, but much to the regret of my ghost-hunting buddies I am not daring enough to attempt this form of divination. It's just too creepy for me. However, my daughter, Tammy (who trances easily) and my dear ghost-hunting friend, Lisa, will probably attempt this some night. These girls are awesome, fearless investigators who never cease to amaze me. And if they do practice grave-sleeping, you'll probably read about their adventures in another book.

THREE
CEMETERY GHOSTS

When people visit a cemetery they may fail to acknowledge the fact that they are entering a reverent realm of spirits, ghosts, and possibly even entities not of this world.

Because they are mourning, emotional, or perhaps even fearful they are vibrating at a different frequency than usual. It is this vibrational frequency that opens a portal to spiritual contact. It matters little whether you visit a graveyard or cemetery in broad daylight or after midnight, the fact remains that your attitude, beliefs, and vibrational frequencies affect what you may experience.

When we talk about death and cemeteries it seems that the subject of ghosts almost always enters the conversation in one way or another. This is because even in death our loved ones never leave us, and as disembodied souls they are always around us waiting for an opportunity to contact someone, anyone, who is vibrating at their frequency at that particular moment.

Why are ghosts in cemeteries? This was an all-consuming question that kept creeping into my thoughts over the years. Why would they want to be there? After years of investigations and interviews with many people both *dead and alive*, I have arrived at the following conclusions.

1. Murders and heinous crimes have sometimes taken place in cemeteries and graveyards around the world and still do to this day. Confusion, anger, and even revenge are a few of the things that would keep a ghost connected to the cemetery as its last place of existence. In order to move forward it must first resolve the issues of its personal views of spirituality, whether it be religious or

of an occult mindset. Perhaps they are seeking closure and eternal rest that eludes them at the spot of their demise, even though their bodies may be buried elsewhere. Late-night visitors may hear inexplicable cries for help or even sad voices. They may see eerie vaporous figures that appear to float among the tombstones. These will be the ghosts who are lost and confused, and perhaps wondering what happened to them as well as their bodies.

2. Natural disasters can certainly prompt many reports of paranormal activity. A good example follows: In Hope, Arkansas there is an old Pioneer/Civil War Cemetery that was struck by a tornado. So forceful was the storm that tall pines and huge oak trees were uprooted, causing grave after grave to be unearthed. Caskets were literally tossed about and piled on top of each other. The destruction was so bad that government officials were called in to re-bury the disinterred bodies. Now, the once peaceful, restful pioneer graveyard is a hotbed of activity. Many of the soldiers were re-buried in mass graves. Sadly this has created energy pockets of frustration and even anger for their ghostly counterparts. Eerie voices can be heard, and odd luminous balls of light are frequently seen floating among the graves; perhaps bemoaning the fact that they weren't allowed to rest in peace.

3. An even more sinister reason is grave robbers and vandals with little or no respect for the deceased. This would anger any deceased soul.

4. Not everything seen and heard in a cemetery is necessarily a ghost. Because cemeteries and graveyards were often established near a *portal* to energize the souls of the dead, many nature spirits, elementals, alien visitors, and creatures such as Bigfoot can just as easily be lurking in the shadows or even in the bright light of day. One such event took place in Rondo Cemetery on a bright sunny afternoon. I was taking pictures of the cemeteries' tombstones when one particularly tall and stately tombstone caught my attention. Leaning sideways and looking as if it was dangerously close to falling over, it was obvious that severe weather would probably dislodge it. With this in mind I took several pictures to preserve its information and epitaph for genealogical purposes.

When I loaded the pictures on my computer, not only did I have several good pictures of the tombstone, but to my astonishment there was also a monkey-like creature hanging onto the front of it. Its head was turned toward me as if it was watching me. I was amazed, as it certainly hadn't been visible to me at the time I took the pictures. It was about the size of a full-grown monkey with a long tail that was curled upward. It had a quizzical look on its face as if to ask, "What are you doing here?"

Now, if this is possible, and obviously it is, I have to wonder who else or what else was there that I didn't see. Unseen visitors from other realms, ghosts walking along beside me, it actually boggles the mind at times.

After all my years as a paranormal investigator and clairvoyant counselor, I am still amazed at some of the things I encounter. I am reminded of Shakespeare's Horatio when he said, "O'day and night, but this is wondrous," as he was speaking about a ghost. Of course Hamlet's response actually says it all: "And therefore as a stranger give it welcome. There are more things in heaven and earth, Horatio, than are dreamt of in your philosophy." Like Horatio, who was a model of rationality, you may have a hard time grasping the concept of ghosts, and entities from other realms, and although they might not be the kind of beings your philosophies recognize, the fact remains that they do exist.

The following is a list of the ghostly personalities one might encounter in cemeteries and graveyards. I believe that forewarned is forearmed, and hope this information will aid you in your quest to define and categorize the ghostly phenomena you encounter.

1. *Angry Ghosts:* These ghosts may be full of rage. They usually appear when their gravesites have been desecrated or defiled in some way. If their burial plot was unearthed or something was removed from the graveyard, they sometimes surface to express their displeasure.

2. *Bereavement Ghosts:* These are the most common and stay near to say hello or goodbye to their loved ones. They may show up only once, or several times over a period of years. Their desire is to let everyone know that they are okay, safe, or no longer in pain. They know that the gravesite will be visited and arrange to be there at the appropriate times for contact.

3. *Confused Ghosts:* These ghosts are not aware that they are dead. They are oblivious to the fact that they are no longer alive. They realize that they are different; however they may not understand why no one can hear or see them. They will appear confused, lost, and very frustrated.

4. *Curious Ghosts:* These ghosts appear almost everywhere, including cemeteries. They are adjusting to their new existence and may actually like it, especially if they have mastered their skills of manifestation and communication. They interact with others and actually want to make positive contacts.

5. *Denial Ghosts:* These ghostly entities refuse to acknowledge or accept the fact that they have died. They will remain unable to move on due to their inability to accept the truth of their new-found reality. These ghosts probably lived their embodied lives in denial, and therefore continue to do so even in death.

6. *Emotional Ghosts:* These ghosts acknowledge the fact that they are no longer alive or embodied. However, due to emotional attachments to previous lives and loved ones, they refuse to transition to the next higher dimension. Because of their deep longing and need to stay close to family, friends, and lovers, they may actually remain on earth seeking contact for years.

7. *Fearful Ghosts:* These ghosts are afraid to move forward. Religious or cultural conditioning may have created a deeply embedded fear of judgment or hell. They fear the outcome of their actions and dread the transition

so much that they hide from themselves as well as everyone else. They only contact others of their particular religion or cultural background, in the hope that they can understand what is happening to them.

8. *Jealous Ghosts:* Although rare, there are ghosts whose jealousy and possessive nature interferes with their ability to move forward and accept their spiritual evolvement. They may become attached to lovers or spouses and therefore are reluctant to let go. They can be very difficult to deal with as they become more and more possessive. In life they were probably very controlling and manipulative, and unwilling to let go of their insecurities.

9. *Mischievous Ghosts:* These ghosts are tricksters. They enjoy playing practical jokes on unsuspecting visitors, especially ghost hunters and investigators. They will interact as long as they have an adequate energy supply to draw from. They will move things around, hide things, tug at your hair, give you goose bumps, and touch you. They are basically harmless. However, late at night in a darkened graveyard they can seem scary indeed.

10. *Motivated Ghosts:* these ghosts are very active. They usually have unfinished business to take care of. Perhaps their life ended too soon and they were unable to accomplish their goals. If the death was unexpected, they may never have closure until they have interacted with someone for the purpose of ending their quest. They may have a message that needs to be de-

livered, an apology to make or a confession that needs to be heard.

11. *Playful Ghosts:* These are usually the ghosts of children who have transitioned without fear. They like to giggle and laugh and are very curious about everyone who enters the cemetery. They choose to stay close to their gravesite and usually enjoy company. Most are happy and have adjusted to their new dimension. They may try to assist newly deceased children in their understanding of death and vibrational transformation. They may also try to tell you their names as a method of contact with you.

12. *Sad Ghosts:* These ghosts will appear to be overwhelmed at the loss of their physical bodies. They will be sensed as a depressing energy. They may be remorseful, crying, moaning, and projecting the sounds of someone in emotional pain. Suicides would fall into this category as well as ghosts who may regret their actions, especially if they have caused someone pain and suffering, or caused someone else's death.

13. *Vengeful Ghosts:* These ghosts have a plan and are working that plan. They are not as angry as they are dedicated to resolving their objective. If they have been murdered, or their death was caused by malicious intent they may be, literally dead set upon revenge. They can be very dangerous, especially if their vengeance is misplaced. Just because they are ghosts doesn't mean that they have all the answers.

14. *Ghostly Guardians:* These ghosts have been buried with a specific purpose in mind: to protect the people interred in their cemetery from vandals, grave robbers, souvenir seekers, and evil entities. They are usually the ghosts of the first person buried in the cemetery. However, they may also exist as a result of being buried alive for that specific purpose.

15. *Protective Ghosts:* These ghosts are benevolent and welcome guests in any cemetery. They are very protective of people they resonate with, and try to comfort mourners and visitors. They will try to guide people to the gravesite they are searching for and will do their best to offer comfort and protection to everyone who enters their domain.

If you have never seen, heard, or felt the presence of a ghost, undoubtedly the prospect will seem unreal and you may justifiably doubt their existence. However, what you may have perceived as unreal may suddenly become surreal once you encounter a ghostly presence. You will never doubt their existence again. You will probably be unable to escape the fascination and mystery of ghosts who reside in other dimensions, yet mysteriously within our own.

Contrary to what most people believe about ghosts, they may actually be seen as daytime apparitions as well as nighttime ghosts. Perhaps the fact that more people see ghosts at night can be attributed to the moon. The moon's cycles facilitate all spirit activity. It stands to reason that it would also enhance the manifestation of ghosts and spirits.

The full moon and the new moon are extremely powerful. They can generate vibrational frequencies that create immense geomagnetic fields. The moon's phases also greatly affect our personal energy field (aura), by allowing us to perceive our reality on new expanded levels.

The waxing and waning of the moon also plays a key role in spirit activity, allowing ghost hunters to record and photograph anomalies and ghosts; often with startling results. Magnetic storms may also have a very profound affect on paranormal activity as well.

In closing this chapter, I would like to mention a very crucial aspect of maintaining contact with a ghost once an encounter has occurred. First of all, when someone sees a ghost or feels a ghostly presence nearby, the best thing they can do is stand as still as possible, relax, and use their innate senses of sight, hearing, and smell to comprehend what the ghost is trying to convey.

This may seem to be a laughable request. Once fear gets a firm grip on your imagination, the only other instinct that will surface will probably be *Survival*, followed by *Run*, close on the heels of *Don't look back!*

If you can suppress those thoughts and feelings and just stand still for a minute or two, you will probably be rewarded with an amazingly direct ghostly communication. This will be possible because of your willingness to allow the ghost to come to you on its own terms. It will have successfully manipulated the magnetic vibrational energy frequencies surrounding it in order to manifest. If you were to walk or run toward it, you would no doubt disturb its newly acquired energy form, in which case it would probably disappear or just dissipate into thin air. Of course the chances of reconnecting with it would probably be gone and any communication or messages lost as well.

I believe that most ghosts want to interact with us on a positive level. However, it is up to us to find new, better, and even safer ways to communicate with them. There is a fine line between fear and acceptance; once removed, a new dimensional reality will emerge.

When this happens, ghosts who were once human, and humans who were once ghosts or spirits, will be able to close the gap between fear and acceptance forever.

FOUR
EXTRAORDINARY
CEMETERIES

A book about cemeteries and ghosts would not be complete without a chapter on weird, odd, and unusual cemeteries, and the ghosts who haunt them. These unique cemeteries have their own personal ghosts and paranormal anomalies—different yet somewhat alike in manifestation.

In these strange, often ignored and sometimes hidden cemeteries the atmosphere will feel different. The tombstones and their inscriptions may be fantastic, elaborate, cryptic, mysterious, or simply nonexistent. Unusual deaths may be depicted by bizarre symbols, designs, and inscriptions.

Ghost hunting and investigations in these odd cemeteries can be either interesting and exciting or sad and gloomy experiences. Either way, ghost hunting in these graveyards will evoke a need to understand the lives of the deceased and the circumstances of their deaths. As we learn more about their existence we ultimately learn more about ourselves in the process. Whatever a ghostly encounter reveals, we should try to understand the ghosts with compassion and sincerity, and accept that they were people too.

What do these unique cemeteries say about the people who are buried there? What do they reveal about their spirit and the communities they lived in? These questions and many more will surface as you wander among the amazing tombstones. Some of these cemeteries are extremely interesting and some may be frightening, mainly because the ghosts who reside there all have their own unique personalities, just as we do.

Although *they* scare us, I am sure that *we* startle them just as much by entering their private domain. They may greet visitors pleasantly or they may scare unsuspecting ghost hunters for trespassing in their sacred space. Every ghost and every anomaly is different, yet all are bound by one common factor—they prove without a doubt that death is not necessarily the final ending.

With this in mind, let's explore the netherworld of odd, curious, and fantastic cemeteries of the dead.

CIRCUS CEMETERY

Hugo, Oklahoma, once known as Circus City, is a designated resting place for circus performers both dead and alive.

The Kelly-Miller and Carson and Barnes Big Tops came to Hugo for the winter and unfortunately some of the performers became ill and couldn't continue their journeys under the Big Top. When this occurred they were interred in "Showman's Rest Cemetery" (www.roadsideamerica.com), which is located within the boundaries of the larger Mt. Olivet Cemetery that encompasses several acres of attractive green landscape. Showman's Rest was established in the 1960s when the Elephant Man, John Carroll, created a trust fund for the cemetery. The cemetery was previously known as the Burgoyne Cemetery. The rectangular burial area for the circus performers is defined by multiple granite monuments, each topped with a small elephant statue. The first impressive monument you will probably notice is a gigantic tombstone with a performing elephant etched on it. Underneath it is engraved "A Tribute to all Showmen under God's Big Top."

Just as impressive and overwhelming is the tombstone of the "Tall Showman Ringmaster, John Strong." It is an extraordinary ten-foot tall monument and depicts the life-size ringmaster in his full circus attire including the top hat that characterized his vibrant personality. The back of the tombstone reads, "The man with more friends than Santa Claus."

Many of the tombstones carry the name of Miller including the founder of Kelly-Miller, "Obert." Beautifully etched on the tombstone is the main entrance to a circus including the ticket booth. Miller's son, the late D. R. Miller, is buried here also and his tombstone, although simple, is very elegiac; "Dun Rovin."

As you stroll among the serene gravesites you will immediately sense the nostalgic sights, sounds, and smells of the circus; colorful clowns, carousel music, and the unmistakable smell of popcorn and cotton candy. You can almost feel the excitement of the circus as you gaze at the tombstones. These monuments are a glorious representation of their lives, as well as a tribute to their performances under the Big Top. From the animal trainers and performers to the ringmaster, the circus comes alive, albeit in death. The excitement builds as you visit one gravesite after another.

John Carroll, an elephant trainer for thirty-five years, is portrayed standing on the head of an elephant and waving to the crowds.

An interesting wagon wheel monument for Ted Bowman reads on the back, "Nothing Left But Empty Popcorn Sacks and Wagon Tracks." Jack B. Moore's headstone is actually carved into a model of a Big Top Tent.

Also at Mt. Olivet cemetery are the gravesites of three world championship rodeo cowboys, the original Marlboro

Man, and one of the Buster Brown Midgets. The Brown Shoe company hired more than twenty midgets to represent them. They were dressed in Little Lord Fauntleroy outfits and portrayed the five-year-old boy "Buster Brown." Also buried in Mt. Olivet is William Edmond Ansley, who portrayed the character for twenty-seven years.

Not far from the cemetery on Kirk Road is the actual winter home of the circuses. At one time Circus City boasted as many as fifteen different shows. In the summer there are various circus wagons and tractor trailers out on the grounds and in the winter the second largest herd of elephants in the country rests up for the next season. Hugo is the winter headquarters to at least three of America's largest circuses. Carson and Barnes, Kelly-Miller Brothers, and Circus Chimera all winter here.

Are there ghosts? You bet! There have been many sightings of ghosts appearing in unusual clothes and circus attire. One particular ghost, a clown, surprises people by sneaking up behind them and honking a horn. Perhaps he is still enjoying the fun and excitement of the circus, albeit from another realm.

Another anomaly that is associated with the cemetery has to do with the energy field surrounding it. Inside the cemetery boundaries, the temperature is at least ten degrees cooler than outside. I have felt this myself and the difference in temperature is remarkable, especially on a very hot summer day. For this reason local people use the cemetery path as a walking trail. The ghosts and spirits of the Showman's Rest and Mount Olivet Cemeteries have helped to create pleasant surroundings for themselves, as well as all the family and friends who come to visit. If it is possible that a cemetery is fun to visit, this is the one.

UNDERWATER CEMETERY

Fishing the cemetery can be a very haunting experience.

El Salto Lake is a mysterious lake located seventy miles northeast of Mazatlan, Mexico. The lake offers bass fishing as well as an eerie landscape. It is part of the Rio Elota River and covers approximately twenty-four thousand surface acres, with a depth of two hundred twenty-five feet at the dam.

El Salto Lake is a scenic area located deep within the heart of the Sierra Madre Occidental mountain range. The lower edge of El Salto consists of steep rocky banks with very sharp drops. The lake also has amazing water clarity. It has literally hundreds of brush-cluttered points and ridges that harbor more double-digit bass than any lake in the world.

Does it sound like the perfect place for bass fishing? Maybe, maybe not.

What makes El Salto Lake interesting is that it contains the flooded ruins of two towns and a couple of ancient cemeteries whose intriguing tombstones rise gracefully from beneath the mysterious depths of the lake (www.flickr.com).

Throughout history huge dams, lakes, and reservoirs have been created to benefit states, towns, and rural communities. However, the wheels of progress and the powers that be seldom stop to consider the emotional losses to the people involved.

Recently a photograph rejuvenated my interest in these lost cemeteries and tombstone memorials for those who have died but couldn't remain where they were interred, or if not moved were left to slumber in watery graves. Ghost hunters are well aware that ghosts often become very active after their resting places have been disturbed.

Suspicious mists, voices from beneath the water, eerie forms floating on the surface, and luminous figures rising from the water have probably sent many unsuspecting fishermen, boaters, or swimmers into shock. Do such places exist? Are they surrounded by legends and folklore about ghosts and eerie apparitions? Yes, of course.

Perhaps you will find this information intriguing, especially if you are a ghost hunter or a bass fisherman. Searching out these submerged towns may reveal answers to local folklore and urban legends that may have surfaced from the watery graves of the unknown.

In the United States, state codes and laws regarding flooding cemeteries or burial grounds usually declare that a proper notice should be issued prior to the creation of an artificial lake or reservoir that will inundate a cemetery. The names of the buried should be listed in an attempt to notify existing relatives. Then the relatives of all the people who are buried in the designated cemetery would have the opportunity to contact the power companies with their proposals in regard to the disposition of the remains of their deceased family members or ancestors. If no one comes forward, then the power companies carry on with their plans, deciding whether or not the bodies from a cemetery or graveyard should be reinterred or remain where they are. Given the cost of relocating an entire cemetery full of bodies, we can guess what their decision would be. Sadly, this practice happens much more than people realize.

PHANTOM CEMETERIES

A remarkable paranormal phenomenon exists in the form of phantom cemeteries.

My nephew, Joel, had a puzzling experience while hunting wild hogs with four of his friends. They were walking deep in the woods when they came upon a small overgrown graveyard nestled in a ticket of pine trees. They were surprised to see that although there were pine trees inside the graveyard, as well as surrounding it, there were no pine needles on the ground. The men took a little time to walk among the graves. There were at least thirty or more tombstones dating from the early 1800s. One member of the group took a several photos of the cemetery. It was a clear day, but when the pictures were developed they were amazed to see that the tombstones didn't show up on film. All that showed was the dry dusty dirt of the cemetery grounds, and a deep foggy mist covering the exact spot where all the tombstones were photographed.

They continued their trek, and after a day of hunting set out for their four-wheelers. On their way back they returned on the same path that they had taken into the woods.

Joel, who was still intrigued with the isolated graveyard, was anxious to revisit the gravesites. Much to his surprise, when they arrived at the area where they had seen the graveyard, it wasn't there.

The men were confused, thinking they must have strayed away from their original path. So they backtracked and searched again for the small graveyard. It was nowhere to be found. Did Joel actually see a graveyard? Of course he did. Did they photograph the tombstones? Yes, they did. But where was the secluded graveyard?

Did Joel and his hunting buddies experience a time slip; where time doesn't seem to flow in the way we normally perceive it? Because our perception of time is limited and subject to our routine lives, we tend to deny experiences that are out of the ordinary or challenge our personal view of reality. When portals to the past or future open up right in front of our eyes it can appear as one of the most bizarre and disorienting things we have ever experienced. Once you have had an experience such as this, the memory of the phenomena will always remain with you.

The following story is yet another example of a mysterious phantom cemetery.

In 1979 an eight-year-old boy traveled overseas with his family to visit his mother's relatives in Scotland. The family lived in a small town situated in a secluded valley. Behind his grandmother's house was a very large wooded area. The road next to her house was not very wide and narrowed into a meandering trail through these woods. As was a family custom, the entire family would start the day off by taking long leisurely walks up this winding pathway.

One morning while on one of these family outings, the boy decided to lag behind and enjoy the scenery. While walking alone he came upon a small cemetery on the side of the trail. He was curious as to why he had not seen it before, wondering how he could have missed it. He decided to walk inside and look around. He was eerily affected by the fact that almost all of the tombstones belonged to children, many of whom were his age or younger. He clearly remembers that the dates were from the early 1800s.

Excited about his discovery, he rushed to find his family and tell them all about the odd cemetery. They didn't seem very interested and basically ignored him. He was very confused, even more so when walking back down the trail he couldn't find the cemetery again. It just wasn't there.

Twenty years later this young man returned to Scotland to visit his grandmother's gravesite. While he was in the cemetery where she was laid to rest, he noticed that graves from the WWII era and even earlier suffered weather damage, and it was actually difficult to read what was engraved on them. Seeing these tombstones brought back vivid memories of the headstones in the small cemetery he had encountered as a child. He remembered that the inscriptions he had read were very distinct and easy to read.

This experience has always remained with him, and he has often wondered if the cemetery itself was a ghost!

An interesting aspect of these phantom cemetery stories is that the people involved actually stepped into another dimension when they walked beyond the boundaries of the cemeteries. Barriers of time and space were removed. Even more intriguing is the fact that they experienced no ill effects from their journey into the unknown.

BODY PARTS CEMETERY

I couldn't resist adding this small article which was discovered in the *Dallas Morning News* by Chad Lewis, author of *Hidden Headlines of Texas*.

Denison has a most peculiar graveyard; in fact it is probable that there is not another cemetery of the kind to be found in the state. The burial ground is a small plot of land lying north and immediately adjoining the Missouri, Kansas, and Texas freight depot and is for the interment of hands, legs, fingers, and such other parts of human beings as are mashed or mutilated by the cars in such a manner as necessitates amputation.

In the Missouri, Kansas, and Texas yard in this city and among its hundreds of miles of tracks north, south, and west of the city accidents are frequently occurring, and a large number of those are forwarded here for medical and surgical treatment. The freight building is used for such purposes and the vacant lot north of the platform is used as a depository for amputated substances. Two weeks ago the legs of little Johnny Wells were interred in this peculiar graveyard and this morning the right foot of E. R. McCain found a grave at the same place.

I couldn't help but wonder what kinds of ghosts or paranormal activity, if any, would be encountered in a graveyard of this type. Would a ghost return to reclaim their missing limbs? Very interesting, indeed!

FIVE
CEMETERY GUARDIANS

Edgar Allen Poe wrote in his macabre *The Premature Burial*, that "to be buried alive was beyond the most terrific of these extremes which has ever befallen to the lot of mere mortality." He added that "the boundaries which divide life from death are at least shadowy and vague." And he concluded with "who shall say when one ends and the other begins?" Could he have been writing about cemetery guardians?

What are cemetery guardians? How did they come into existence? The answers are as bizarre and terrifying as Poe's tales of misery, death, and the mysteries of life.

After years of investigations and paranormal research in cemeteries and graveyards, I became intrigued and fascinated by the seemingly menacing orbs, light anomalies, and energy balls that are sometimes seen, heard, and even photographed on occasion. Some of these eerie anomalies are able to project a fierce image to frighten people away. But why? This question led me to explore and research these ominous anomalies.

Cemetery guardians are protectors of the disembodied spirits who seem to linger in graveyards and cemeteries around the world. An old English legend tells us that the ghost of the first person buried in a newly established cemetery or graveyard was responsible for guarding it against the devil, and was therefore imbued with special powers. Legends and folklore say that at times a black dog would be buried alive in the cemetery before any human being, so that it would take on the ominous task of guarding the cemetery. In the early 1800s in some countries, including rural America, whenever a new graveyard or cemetery was established, it was customary to bury some unfortunate victim alive in the first grave so that a ghostly guardian could be created. However, the high probability of people actually being buried alive due to medical ignorance could account for many of the graveyard ghosts and guardians still around today. As cemetery guardians, their purpose is to frighten off anyone—*dead or alive*—who might enter to disturb the peaceful repose of the dead.

Some guardians are benevolent, quietly watching over the cemeteries they have inherited. However, others may present themselves as disturbed, angry ghosts. Who could blame them? They were forced into guardian status against their will. They wander impatiently, watching for unwelcome visitors in the graveyard. They linger ready and waiting to frighten everyone who ventures into their cemetery. They may manifest as glowing orbs, indefinable light forms, or menacing ecto-mist. They may appear, disappear, and then reappear, over and over, in an attempt to frighten people away. And most of the time they are very successful.

Cemetery guardians seem to dart about, moving swiftly from tombstone to tombstone as if checking on their charges. These glowing orbs have been witnessed and photographed in an array of colors with golden yellow, green, blue, and red being the most prominent.

My introduction to one such glowing cemetery guardian came through my niece, Christy, who is also a member of our ghost hunting team. She had a terrifying experience in a local cemetery late one night. I have included her story of the green ball of light that frightened her on not one, but two separate occasions.

GREEN CEMETERY GUARDIAN

Christy and one of her high school friends were driving around late one Saturday night, just hanging out, talking about school, and sharing secrets. Suddenly, as they passed a cemetery, they noticed a strange light shining from deep within. They watched closely as it moved slowly among the tombstones. The cemetery is right next to a large church and the parking lot is well lighted, so they decided to park there and see what happened next.

Thinking that it was probably just the glow from a nearby streetlight or the reflection on a tombstone, they had almost decided to leave when suddenly the light began to move about erratically. At this point Christy decided she wanted to get a closer look, but her friend wouldn't budge from the car. Being the fearless investigator she is, Christy got out of the car alone and walked slowly into the darkened cemetery. She hadn't gone very far when she heard a car door close and she smiled as she realized that her friend preferred her company to sitting alone in the dark car.

Together they slowly followed the green ball of light until it came to rest on top of a tombstone. Christy reached out for the light and at that exact moment she heard someone whisper something, but was unable to make out what was being said. Then suddenly they heard a loud booming sound and the street light went out. Both girls ran to the car as fast as they could. Frightened by the thunderous sound, Christy later regretted that she hadn't looked at the name on the tombstone.

Of course, once someone has had an electrifying paranormal encounter it is almost impossible to forget it, and this was no exception. About a month later Christy felt she just had to tell someone and confided in her sister Becky, who she was pretty sure wasn't going to think she was crazy. Becky didn't know what to think at first, but that was about to change soon enough.

Late one evening after an outing, Christy and her family were returning home. Their father, who is my very psychic brother Ricky, decided to take a longer way home and turned on the road that passed the cemetery where the girls had seen the green orb. Christy was excited and couldn't keep her secret any longer. She revealed her terrifying experience to everyone in the car.

Her father decided to dispel her fears, and perhaps understand for himself what had *really happened*, by stopping at the cemetery. They sat in the car for quite some time, watching and waiting, but it seemed that nothing was going to happen. Afraid that no one believed her, she telepathically begged for the green ball of light to return once more. Suddenly, there it was! Before anyone could stop them, Christy and her two sisters, Becky and Samantha, were out of the car and following the green light across the cemetery.

The orb appeared to be about the size of a grapefruit and it moved in a zigzag manner across the cemetery. Christy knew exactly where it was headed, and she and her sisters huddled together as they moved closer and closer toward the green light.

Ricky had retrieved his flashlight from the trunk of the car and was headed rapidly toward his headstrong daughters. He watched as the light did just as Christy said it had before, and came to rest on the top of the same tombstone. What happened next was both unbelievable and terrifying at the same time.

Just as they reached the tombstone, Christy heard the voice again, and this time she also heard a baby crying. Boom! There was another thunderous noise, just as before. It sent the girls screaming and their father racing toward them at breakneck speed.

Christy and Samantha were running side by side, looking backward to make sure that Becky was right behind them. She wasn't. She was lying face down on the ground and screaming. She yelled that someone had grabbed her ankles and was holding her down.

The two girls ran back to her and attempted to pull her away. They pulled as hard as they could, but something or someone was pulling just as hard to keep her there. Just as their father reached them, they gave one more forceful yank, and with their adrenalin rushing they were able to free her from the grasp of an unseen, unknown captor. They all hit the ground and with the help of their father managed to scramble to their feet and run back to the safety of the car.

Their father ordered them to never return to that cemetery again. They didn't. However, ten years later our investigative team, Ricky, Christy, and I went there to investigate the glowing green cemetery guardian. I can assure you that it was no less exciting this time.

Intent upon solving this mystery, we showed up with all our equipment, ready to conduct a very thorough investigation. At first, the night was still and calm. However, things quickly turned chaotic as darkness enveloped us.

First, orbs and energy streaks began to appear. Our cameras revealed weird pictures of fellow ghost hunters as they appeared to be floating outside their bodies, creating a doppelganger effect. This affected everyone, and we should have been prepared for what was to come. My niece's boyfriend, Joel, was with us on his first cemetery investigation. It seemed he had been singled out for the experience of a lifetime. As we walked through the cemetery photographing, recording, and documenting what we saw and heard, he suddenly called out to me.

"Hey, Melba, my hair is standing up all over my body! Wha-what does that mean?" he began to stammer. He was beginning to sound really perplexed, so I turned to explain to him how energy fields interact with us. However, what I saw with my own eyes gave me such a start that I was unable to speak at first. An enormous, thick green mist was approaching him at rapid speed. It appeared to have a white-hot center and was apparently taking on form. I grabbed my camera tightly and took an amazing photograph. The mist was headed straight toward our new investigator.

"Oh my gosh," I thought, "what are we going to do?" Or worse yet, "What is it going to do?" Questions flooded my mind as I called to the other team members. Together we all ran toward Joel, not knowing what to expect or what we were going to do.

Suddenly we all felt as if we had entered an electrical storm. Our hair was standing up on end and everyone felt varying degrees of anxiety, including goose bumps, headaches, ears ringing, and nausea. Then just as suddenly as it appeared it was gone. It simply disappeared into the early morning air. We all agreed it was time to go! Whatever or whoever was there had accomplished its purpose. If its purpose was to scare us away, it had succeeded. But what exactly had we experienced? Although we meant no disrespect and certainly were not intent upon disturbing anything, we somehow were perceived as a threat. I believe that a cemetery guardian was carrying out its purpose of guarding the gravesites of those who are interred there.

The majority of graveyard ghost stories that involve voices being heard and ecto-mist or full apparitions being seen could very well be the work of a cemetery guardian. Cemeteries gain a reputation for being haunted for many reasons, including grave robberies, mysterious unmarked graves, weird statuary, and cemetery disturbances. However, there could be a very straightforward reason, one that has been around for centuries; a *cemetery guardian*.

Whenever a graveyard guardian is involved, its presentation of energy is usually quite different. They are connected to glowing balls (orbs) of light, and are usually described as ranging in size from a softball to a volleyball. They appear to have an electrifying glow about them, as if surging with energy. They have been reported moving slowly and deliberately among the tombstones and at times appear to linger or stop completely at a particular tombstone or gravesite.

Also associated with cemetery guardians are the loud booming sounds that have been heard, and I have personally experienced these myself. The sound is similar to a sonic boom, but at a lower volume. Perhaps as the cemetery guardian absorbs energy from its surrounding, it creates this effect.

These mysterious glowing lights, shimmering with bright colors and vibrating energy, have been witnessed for decades in graveyards and cemeteries. Elusive and ghostly, they are no less frightening today than they were centuries ago.

RED GRAVEYARD GUARDIAN

On the outskirts of Texarkana is situated a very isolated, secluded slave cemetery. Abandoned after years of non-use, it has since become overgrown and mostly forgotten. Shrouded by huge live oak and cedar trees, it is almost impossible to see from the road. Actually it sits off a narrow side road deep in the woods. At the front and near the center is a magnificent oak tree with a huge extended limb. The tree is well over two hundred years old. Local legend claims it was used as a hanging tree, and tales and rumors persist about the tree and the unfortunate people who died there.

It seems that this particular cemetery has been plagued with atrocities ever since it was established in the mid 1800s. Other than the infamous hanging tree, there are also rumors, which have proven to be fact, that witches actually preformed rituals in the graveyard on certain nights during the year, and possibly still do today. Such activities may attract negative energies to the location and, of course, could play a big part in the paranormal phenomena that is experienced by unsuspecting visitors. Good witch or bad witch, it doesn't matter which; they can still set up a vibrational frequency that could be disruptive to the peace of those who are buried there. Also, without a doubt, any disembodied spirit who has chosen to linger in the graveyard will be eerily affected as well.

As if the hangings and witchcraft weren't enough to un-settle the fated graveyard, the Ku Klux Klan also invaded the graveyard. They were actually witnessed performing a secret meeting among the tombstones. They had a roaring fire going and were chanting as they walked around it. Their chanting and circling became more frenzied as the night wore on. They were clothed in white capes and wore tall, pointed, white hats. This occurred in the late 1970s and may or may not continue today. The person who accidentally stumbled upon this meeting was scared beyond belief and wishes to remain anonymous, hoping never to see such a sight again. With all of these activities attached to the graveyard, is it any wonder that it displays paranormal activities?

After hearing eye-witness accounts and reports of ghosts, witches, strange noises, and a huge red ball of light that chases people from the graveyard, of course we had to investigate. I, for one, was extremely interested in the glowing red orb, so we put together a group of *seasoned* investigators to record, photograph, and document these unusual activities.

We decided to begin after midnight and arrived with equip-ment ready to conduct an investigation into the supernatu-ral realm of this old slave graveyard. For a while everything seemed calm and we noticed nothing out of the ordinary. This gave us an opportunity to become more familiar with the graveyard. There were tombstones deeply embedded in the ground and some of the graves had sunken badly. Years of ne-glect coupled with the ravages of time and weather had created a truly forlorn place. A great sadness seemed to permeate the entire graveyard. I began to feel unusual emotions. Although I have felt emotional before while in cemeteries, I had never felt such intensity. Of course this should have been my first clue that everything was not as it should be. It was unnerving to stand there in the dark. I felt like something or someone was watching me all the time, and I was very uneasy.

It wasn't long until orbs of every size began showing up on our digital camera screens. Suddenly, we began to hear noises that couldn't be attributed to any known wildlife. We also heard rustling noises in the woods behind the tree line. This too was beginning to make us a little anxious.

At one point, I was walking back to the car alone when I sensed something staring down at me. It seemed to come from a tree in front of me. Thinking that it was possibly an owl or raccoon I continued on. I could hear that my team-mates were nearby and close behind me so I really wasn't fearful. However, my false sense of security was soon shattered. As I raised my gaze upward to the tree ahead of me, what I saw so startled me that I tripped and nearly feel flat on my face. Then I stumbled backward as a huge red orb at least as big as a basketball loomed ahead of me. It was glowing red with two smaller nucleus-like eyes and I swear it had a tongue hanging out from below its eyes. I regained my composure long enough to snap a picture. It appeared on my camera screen as a dark red orb with very pronounced eyes and a tongue that *was* hanging out. I stood mesmerized as three team members approached. Sharon, a very experienced ghost hunter, was also able to capture it on her camera. After Sharon's last camera flash, the red glow diminished and was gone. I stood there rooted to the very spot where I first saw the guardian and I seemed to be unable to move. Oblivious to my plight, Sharon rushed to show the others what she had captured on her camera.

Two team members stayed with me and I was grateful for their presence. At the time I didn't realize just how thankful I was to become. Suddenly, we heard footsteps all around us. We could hear leaves being crunched and it was clear to us that several unseen entities were forming a circle around us. We could feel the movement as they circled us and the energy gained in intensity. To be honest, now I was scared, really scared, and so were my fellow teammates. We looked at each other and acknowledged that we were experiencing the same thing. Well, now we had two choices. We could stay and experience the paranormal activity, or run! Of course we opted for the latter and made a dash for the car. It didn't take long for the others to pick up on our panic and follow suit. Having had their own experiences, they too had decided that enough was enough. Anything else was better left for another time.

Just as we were preparing to leave, our attention was diverted back to the graveyard by a creepy sound. Damn, there it was again. Glaring down at us from a huge tree limb was that enormous red ball of pulsating energy. I am sure it was pleased that it had frightened away yet another group of people. To be honest, I didn't feel quite as knowledgeable or professional as I had when we first arrived. Never knowing what to expect on a ghost hunt or paranormal investigation can be very unnerving at times.

Still, I was able to see and photograph yet another graveyard guardian to add to my research. I was very excited about this, and even more so after we were safely away from the graveyard and its ominous protector.

Strange cemetery anomalies such as colored lights, weird noises, and glowing tombstones have been reported for centuries. Although sometimes there doesn't seem to be any logical explanation for them, they are still seen, felt, and photographed with such consistency that their existence is unquestionable.

Ghost hunters, in their attempts to understand paranormal phenomena, have been able to document and define these anomalies. Our ability to record these mysterious anomalies may pave the way for future scientific exploration, thereby helping everyone understand and accept the fact that we, as human beings, are energy responding to spiritual guidelines and celestial vibrations.

The next story reveals yet another aspect of cemetery guardians to help shed light on who and what they are, as well as their purpose.

ENERGIZED CEMETERY GUARDIAN

Rose Hill Cemetery is old, and steeped in history. During the daytime it is a peaceful, serene environment. Lovely old weathered tombstones are surrounded by magnificent spreading magnolias and large oak trees. It is laid out in sections and well tended. However, at night it doesn't even begin to resemble the tranquil atmosphere of the daylight hours.

We have been there often and on several occasions we witnessed a small green orb that seemed to stay on the left side of the cemetery, near the middle, and always seemed to wander to the back section and to one grave in particular. Two of our investigators, Lisa and Tammy, decided to follow it one night, and it actually seemed to enjoy its game of hide and seek. We had a news reporter with us that night and although he was definitely a skeptic, he too became intrigued with the mysterious anomaly. The green light hid first behind one tombstone and then another until it arrived once again at the back of the cemetery where it would blink out completely. It appeared to be benevolent and playful and gave us little cause for concern.

However, I always felt a little uneasy about it. I think that if something looks like a duck and walks like a duck...or in this case, a *cemetery guardian*, it probably is! Well, guess what? I was right. It was a cemetery guardian, and it revealed its true nature to us before the night was over.

We had decided to conclude our investigation and leave when things suddenly went from peaceful and calm to chaotic. We were taking some last-minute group pictures, when we noticed on our camera screens that some of our members were covered in a faint green mist. After that it began to show up beside us, around us, behind us, and even totally covering some of us in the pictures. The air felt cooler and the spine-tingling intensity of the energy was amazing. Suddenly, the mist attached itself to Gary, one of our investigators, and actually started to follow him around. We were able to follow him and photograph this amazing phenomenon. Gary was getting really upset by this time and we agreed to leave at his request. What happened next goes to show who was actually in control of the events that transpired. As he dashed for his bright red truck and opened the door, the heavy green mist filled the cab. By this time he was beyond upset. He was scared to death.

Because we couldn't see the mist with our physical eyes, but only through our camera lenses, we anxiously watched our screens until we saw that it was at the back of his truck. When we told him where it was he hastily jumped inside the truck and locked his doors. He raced out of the cemetery with two carloads of investigators and one harried reporter in close pursuit. We all breathed a sigh of relief and were glad to call it a night.

However, we soon noticed that his truck began to swerve in front of us, careening from one side of the road to the other. Then unexpectedly he whipped into the parking lot of a local fire station and jumped out of the truck, screaming! He was frantically brushing himself all over, yelling for us to help get *it* off him. We could clearly see the green mist in the cab of his truck and this time we didn't need the aid of our camera screens. What to do? First, we had to get him away from his truck and make sure that he didn't get back on the road and cause a serious accident. Then we tried unsuccessfully to calm him down. Then Sharon, our fearless leader, actually got up in his truck and sat there demanding that the presence leave immediately. Some of us stood across the road with Gary and the reporter, while other members stood by the truck and supported Sharon's efforts to oust the green guardian. We waited and waited and when it appeared that *it* had finally left, Gary returned rather hesitantly to his truck. We offered to follow him home to assure his safety and he gladly accepted.

The next day the newspaper article chronicled the events of the night and Gary was quoted as saying, "That was the worst experience I have ever had." Investigator Tammy Williams good-naturedly corrected him by saying, "Actually that was the best paranormal experience you could have ever had." We all exploded in laughter when we read this. Looking back, Gary had to admit that it really was the best experience he had ever had, not that he would necessarily want to go through it again.

Yet another electrifying event at the Rose Hill Cemetery can be attributed to the cemetery guardian. On another night four of us decided to go to the cemetery to photograph some statuary for our scrapbook. It was dark and cloudy, and the night seemed to come alive with energy as we entered the old wrought-iron gates. We parked about mid-way so we could walk in all directions leaving us easy access to the car. We have learned to *always expect the unexpected*, and that night proved to be no exception to the rule.

Two team members, Sharon and Kevin, started off in different directions. Christy and I walked together as we took pictures and discussed the cemetery and its supposed ghosts. We turned to see Kevin talking to someone. It was about midnight and this man appeared in the cemetery from seemingly nowhere. He looked as if he could have been homeless, complete with a bag under his arm. Our curiosity aroused, Sharon, Christy, and I walked over to where they were. He began to tell us about the cemetery and who he knew that was buried there, and where they were buried. By this time my intuition had kicked in and I knew that he was not at all who he appeared to be. I was actually getting very nervous, as I wondered exactly what he was up to.

He was pointing out some gravesites where he said his family was buried and we all turned to look in that direction. There was a lovely statue of an angel and it appeared to be engulfed in an ethereal mist. Suddenly a huge orb shot upward out of the ground beside a gravesite that was close to the angel. I was able to photograph that fantastic orb. It was about the size of a beach ball and moving very fast.

Suddenly all three of us started to tingle all over. My face actually began to feel numb, as did Christy's. Realizing that we were standing too close to *something* unnatural, we all backed away hurriedly. Then, just as quickly, all four of us noticed that the mysterious man was no longer with us. In fact he was nowhere to be seen. It was if he had vanished into thin air. A sense of dread permeated my entire body and then it happened. Boom! We heard a thunderous noise that caused all of us to jump and make a mad dash for the car. My hair was standing on end, and by now I felt disoriented. We were all glad Kevin, our resident debunker, was able to drive us out of the cemetery. Of course he went immediately into his debunker mode, trying desperately to analyze the paranormal phenomena we had just experienced. As for the loud boom, he declared that a transformer had blown somewhere. Yeah, right. Something emitted a lot of energy all right, but it wasn't a transformer. It was a cemetery guardian performing his duties, to frighten away anyone and everyone who posed a threat to his cemetery. What an experience! As for the mysterious man, we never saw him again. Was he actually the cemetery's guardian? I believe he was.

So, if you ever find yourself in a cemetery late at night or find yourself frightened by eerie phenomena such as glowing tombstones, uncomfortable sensations, huge colored balls of light, or a mysterious thunderous boom, you will probably have encountered a cemetery guardian. Stay and capitalize on the event if you can. However, I for one will not blame you if you run.

SIX
ALIEN BURIAL

Pre-dating by at least fifty years the Roswell, New Mexico UFO crash and the mysterious removal of its occupants is yet another legend that boasts the burial of an alien navigator who died in an early morning crash. Its spaceship was struck by lightning in stormy weather, forcing it to remain forever in our dimension.

So convincing was the story that in 1976 the Texas Historical Commission erected a historical marker in the cemetery where the alien is presumed to be buried. The official Texas Historical Marker reads:

"This site is also well-known because of the legend that a spaceship crashed nearby in 1897, and the pilot that was killed in the crash was buried here."

This amazingly mysterious story began in the spring of 1897 in the small farming community of Aurora, just a short distance from Fort Worth, Texas, in the southeastern part of Wise County.

The first recorded mention of a town named Aurora came from a traveler who was visiting the nearby town of Boyd's Mill. He wrote that he had heard about a new town that had been established a couple of miles from Boyd's Mill. He remarked that a new store had been erected near the roadside. The town's name, "Aurora," had been suggested by William W. O. Stanfield, because he foresaw the town as something unique to come; something luminous and brilliant was his prediction. He probably had no idea at the time how portentous his statement was to become—or did he? Could he have been aware of a luminous, brilliant portal that allowed access to UFOs as they entered our dimension?

Aurora grew to become a thriving township nestled among majestic oak trees. The gently sloping countryside and beautiful natural landscape attracted many people into the area, adding to the mystique and allure of Aurora.

The town's first settlers arrived to the area in 1854. The town of Aurora was surveyed in 1880 and incorporated in 1882. Marcus Oates donated the land for the town. A well was sunk in the center of a square plot of land. The town grew up around the square as various businesses were established. It soon boasted two hotels, three cotton gins, and a cotton yard; along with a newspaper office, livery stable, brickyard, tannery, shops, and schools. Of course, no town would be complete without its saloons, jail, and ever-present undertaker. Soon Aurora became a booming mecca for travelers, merchants, rural farmers, and cattlemen. In a short time span it grew to be the largest town in Wise County.

However, long before Aurora became a town, a mysterious fraternal lodge was added to the early settler's community. Masonic Lodge #479 was organized on December 17, 1877 and was the only lodge in Texas north of Fort Worth at the time. It was actually in place five years before the town was surveyed, laid out, and incorporated. Does this mean that the town was laid out by the Masons? I believe it does. If this is true, then obviously it plays an extremely important part in the history of Aurora, and the surrounding area. The lodge built a large building in which to hold its secret meetings. Although it cannot be determined exactly when the building was erected, everyone agrees that it was an impressive structure. It sat like an all-seeing eye on a hilltop, commanding a panoramic view of the valley below. It was referred to as the "Masonic Institute," where classes were taught and college work offered by instructors.

The Masonic Lodge remained in Aurora for twenty-two years before it was relocated to the town of Boyd, a mere mile and a half away. At the September 1899 meeting a motion was made to move the lodge to either nearby Rhome or Boyd. The last meeting was held in Aurora in March 1900. However, not only had they agreed to move the fraternal order, they also voted to move the entire building. Perhaps this was done to retain the mysterious energies that were imprinted on the electromagnetic fields contained within the walls.

The April 1900 meeting was held in the Boyd schoolhouse while the original building was being moved. Almost two months elapsed during the moving process and the method used has been a controversial topic of conversation for years. Some said that the building was moved all in one piece, while others surmised that it was dismantled and moved piece by piece. However, according to a longtime resident of Aurora, neither assumption was correct. He proposed that the building be cut into two separate parts and each section moved separately. There wasn't a bridge across the Trinity River at the time so the building had to be rafted across, an enormous undertaking. But why? I for one am puzzled as to why the Masons would invest so much time, and labor to move their building a distance of only a little over a mile. Interesting. Nevertheless, in May 1900 the move was completed and meetings were resumed in the original building in its new permanent location in Boyd, Texas. Could it have anything to do with the 33rd degree parallel? The 33rd degree parallel has long been associated with Freemasonry and this certainly holds true for Aurora, as well. Its Masonic lodge sat only a few miles north of the 33rd parallel. This geographical location holds great importance and could very well hold occult secrets regarding Aurora's mysterious alien burial, eerie paranormal phenomena, and the unique formation created by the four surrounding towns.

The geographical pattern created places Aurora at the center, but of what? This geographical pattern could actually create a powerful energy station with Aurora at the center of the four surrounding towns, which are equidistant to Aurora. Does this represent a pyramid; with the four towns creating the base? If one were overhead looking down, Aurora would be the top of the pyramid and the four smaller towns would outline the base.

The concept of *ley lines* is the catalyst for the 33rd degree parallel. It is well known that certain areas are associated with occult energies and related phenomena—whether negative or positive. Ley lines mark occult, unseen pathways of energy. They can be detected by the use of dowsing rods and sensed by people with clairvoyant abilities, especially at the points where the lines intersect. Points where the energy lines cross or intersect are believed to have a propensity for displaying amazing phenomena, such as ghosts, brilliantly colored lights, hauntings, weird sounds and noises, sightings of nonhuman figures, and even UFOs. Energy at these points is magnified and combined, creating great power sources and possibly even portals. These power points can be accessed for use in rituals, gravitational control factors, ceremonies, healings, and communications, as well as manipulation by aliens and other entities who seek an entrance into our dimension.

There are no early church records in the town of Aurora that might have shed some light on area burials and local activities. There was the Aurora Union Church, but unfortunately the exact date it was established is unknown. The only information on record is that the land for the church was donated by a man named Burch. Inside an old frame building, residents of all faiths met to worship God in the way they understood the scriptures to teach them. Isn't that what the Freemasons believe? And wasn't that an odd concept to be accepted during the religious movements of that day and time? The church was located on a hilltop overlooking the town. Apparently this infamous hilltop was an important location in Aurora—you will read more about it as we go along.

The Masonic Lodge was on the hilltop overlooking the town, a cemetery was situated there for the burial of their dead, and a unique church was also founded there. The people who remained in Aurora throughout the great exodus of families and houses sat on the hilltop and watched the houses go by. One has to wonder who those people really were.

The name Aurora brings up images of mysterious spaceship sightings that occurred around the country during the late 1800s, as well as eye-witness accounts appearing in newspapers throughout cities and communities in America and abroad.

On April 17, 1897 the sleepy town of Aurora with its cryptic name and mysterious Masonic Lodge experienced an earth-shattering event. Suddenly and without warning a spaceship crashed on the outskirts of town. Local resident S. E. Haydon, a cotton buyer and free-lance reporter for the *Dallas Morning News* wrote an electrifying article describing the mysterious unidentified flying airship that had crashed in Aurora. The following is an actual newspaper account of the UFO crash and the fate of its alien navigator (Marrs, 1997).

DALLAS MORNING NEWS
APRIL 17, 1897

A Windmill Demolished It!

About 6 o'clock this morning the early risers of Aurora were astonished at the sudden appearance of the airship which had been sailing through the country.

It was traveling due north, and much nearer the earth than ever before. Evidently some of the machinery was out or order, for it was making a speed of only ten to twelve miles an hour and gradually settling toward the earth. It sailed directly over the public square, and when it reached the north part of town it collided with the tower of Judge Proctor's windmill and went to pieces with a terrible explosion, scattering debris over several acres of land, wrecking the windmill and water tank and destroying the Judge's flower garden.

The pilot of the ship is supposed to have been the only one on board and while his remains were badly disfigured, enough of the original has been picked up to show that he was not an inhabitant of this world.

Mr. T. J. Weems, the United States signal officer at this place and an authority on astronomy, gives it as his opinion that the pilot was a native of the planet

Mars. Papers found on his person—evidently the record of his travels—are written in some unknown hieroglyphics and cannot be deciphered.

The space ship was too badly wrecked to form any conclusions as to its motive power. It was built of an unknown metal, resembling somewhat a mixture of aluminum and silver, and it must have weighed several tons.

The town is full of people today who are viewing the wreck and gathering specimens of the strange metal from the debris. The pilot's funeral will take place at noon tomorrow.

S. E. Haydon

In this country we tend to attribute the frequently reported sightings of UFOs and unusual light anomalies in the skies overhead to weather balloons, experimental airplanes, helicopters, and any number of military craft. However, in the 1800s none of these machines existed. Anything that flew overhead in those days was either a bird of some sort, or possibly the newly developed blimps, but even that would have been an extremely rare sight in America. The only logical explanation was irrefutably the truth: not a bird, not a blimp, but an alien spaceship.

According to local legends and written accounts, the spaceship was totally demolished and the alien pilot was burned and terribly mangled. Although his condition was severe the townsfolk who were at the scene of the crash described him as small, slight, and humanoid in form and structure. Conflicting reports say that the alien navigator either died at the crash scene or was taken by a local doctor to his home and died shortly thereafter. Some reports also say that the doctor kept a diary that chronicled the events of the crash, and that it was later confiscated by military authorities. Either way, the alien apparently died on the day of the crash, and was buried on the next.

Also found among the wreckage of the destroyed space-ship were large pieces of an unusual material. According to eye-witness accounts, the debris was scattered across several acres and some fragments were etched with strange, unfamiliar markings. Much of the scattered debris was later tossed into a well located at the scene of the crash, on Judge Proctor's property.

The people of Aurora gave the alien a proper burial in the Masonic cemetery. Written accounts testify to the fact that the funeral took place at "'high noon" on April 18, 1897, with crowds of onlookers, townsfolk, curiosity seekers, and no doubt members of the enigmatic Masonic Lodge in attendance. Evidently, the alien was buried beneath a huge limb of an old gnarled oak tree in the cemetery. His gravesite is located on the south side of the Aurora cemetery near the front. Is the Aurora cemetery haunted by the ghost of the alien who is buried there, or, are there even more mysterious burials that account for the paranormal activity in the vicinity of the cemetery?

Here perhaps is where the plot thickens. The cemetery where the alien is supposedly buried was owned by the Masonic Lodge and it is well documented that the lodge sold plots for burials. They would have had to bequeath the plot for the alien's interment. My research reveals that there is yet another cemetery located on the hilltop near the Masonic lodge. Could it be that the alien was actually buried in the hilltop cemetery?

It wasn't long before news about the airship crash and the alien burial spread across the Lone Star state like wildfire. People came from all over to Aurora to see what all the excitement was about. The story of the alien was told and retold as gossip and hearsay grew to magnificent proportions, thereby increasing the longevity of the legend.

Evidently a small alien has rested quietly in a well-tended cemetery for exactly one hundred ten years to date. Although a century has elapsed since Haydon's article was published, it is still being read and analyzed with renewed interest whenever and wherever it appears in print. However, Haydon's story of a spaceship was not the only one reported in the late 1800s. Reports came in from various Texas newspapers, including papers from the towns of Whitney, Hillsboro, Waxahachie, Denison, Nacogdoches, Beaumont, and Fort Worth. They all reported a mysterious spaceship which had been sighted in the skies overhead.

Radios were nonexistent in 1897 and newspapers took days, sometimes even weeks, to report the news. Transportation was slow and communication even slower, so the probability of someone faking all the widely spread reports was ridiculous. It didn't happen.

After this initial excitement, news of the UFO crash and the alien burial lay dormant, except for intermittent sightings, for three quarters of a century. In 1973 an investigative reporter stumbled upon a report of the incident and brought it to the attention of a new generation of people seeking the truth of their reality. Soon afterward newspaper articles surfaced with news of the story and once again Aurora entered the spotlight.

Soon the town was swarming with people from the UFO Bureau. This group investigates unidentified flying objects. They proceeded to initiate legal proceedings to exhume the alien's body and were prepared to go to court if necessary to open the grave. This investigation was headed by the director of the International UFO Bureau, Hayden Hewes.

However, things didn't go smoothly and members of the Aurora cemetery association joined together and took a stand to block their efforts. Why? The association's attorney and the judge were in perfect agreement with the members of the cemetery association. To further protect the alien's gravesite, local residents kept a constant vigil at the cemetery. However, the tombstone that supposedly marked the alien's gravesite conveniently disappeared, making it almost impossible for anyone new to the area to find the exact location of the grave.

The mystery of aliens, extraterrestrials, and spaceships is different from other occult phenomena and proof is even harder to document. Proof is oftentimes circumstantial and even when it is backed up by eye-witness accounts and photographs it is still questioned. Too often that same crucial evidence mysteriously disappears, or becomes lost for generations to come.

There are a few interesting facts about the area surrounding Aurora that undoubtedly interconnect with the UFO phenomena of 1897. During a period of less than a year and a half the once booming town of Aurora became a virtual ghost town. How and why remains a mystery even today.

First of all, in 1899, hundreds of townsfolk were suddenly stricken with a disastrous illness that the local doctors diagnosed as "Spotted Fever." Among the families stricken was that of S. E. Haydon, the writer who had reported the airship crash for the *Dallas Morning News*. He lost his wife and two of his four sons. Of the two sons who survived, one was left blind and the other crippled. Many others were frightened into a veritable mass departure. People moved everything they owned including their livestock, and as incredible as it seems, they even moved their homes and businesses. Some fled to Boyd. Some hurried to Rhome. Others still rushed to Boyd's Mill or Briar. Each town was roughly only a mile and half away from Aurora. Does this seem odd to anyone?

We know that the Masonic Lodge was moved to Boyd and a large hotel, the Davis house, was moved to Newark, just beyond Boyd's Mill. I can understand people leaving town for fear that they might catch an illness, but wouldn't one go farther than walking distance, a mile and a half, to avoid catching a life-threatening disease? And didn't people usually burn disease-ridden houses in the hope of stopping the spread of the disease? It seems strange and puzzling that the great exodus would include moving houses and business buildings. Imagine the time and labor, to say nothing of the cost of moving huge buildings for the sake of a mile and a half.

Some accounts say that people sat on the hilltop overlooking the town and watched the houses go by—moving northeast to Rhome, northwest to Boyd, southwest to Briar, and southeast to Boyd's Mill and Newark. Puzzling indeed.

Next, during the same time frame, farmers were plagued with even more problems. Crops suddenly failed to produce the usual yields. For years the bounty had been great, with bumper crops of cotton, wheat, and corn. Three cotton gins were needed to process the cotton. So how did rich soil suddenly fail to produce? How could acres of good soil be contaminated so that it had nothing to offer the farmers who depended on it for survival?

Not only were the crops affected, but what of the wild game, where did they go? Wild hogs which were more than plentiful, deer, squirrel, rabbits, and any number of fowl, gradually disappeared. At this point one has to wonder about the water supplies and the fish in the rivers and streams surrounding Aurora.

Last, but not least by any means, in 1889 the route for the Rock Island Railroad was surveyed and laid out. It was to be built right through Aurora, but something changed and the route originally planned was altered to bypass Aurora, even after the entire proposed track lines had actually been graded. Why?

Despite the appearance of an epidemic, regardless of the crop failures, some people remained in the town, placing their hopes for the future on the railroad. The completion of the railroad was expected in the fall of 1890, but these expectations were never realized. The reason for the failure is controversial. Some people said that there was a lack of funds, while others said that the halt in construction was due to a lawsuit of some sort. At any rate the entire project was abandoned in January 1891.

Aurora was left in a vortex of mystery. The citizens of Aurora who had departed so rapidly were afraid and never returned home. Why? The houses, businesses, hotels, and buildings were all gone. Why? The land that had once been so productive was now dormant, and the railroad now followed a new route. Why? There seems to be no rhyme or reason to the mysterious death of the once illustrious Aurora, Texas.

Keeping secrets always involves energy losses for the people who keep them. This leads to illnesses, depression, and mental confusion. When the power and awareness of the truth is being withheld, manipulation is the result. Manipulation then creates domination or submission, which also destroys trust and guarantees inner fear. This of course leads to collective fear. This collective fear could then prompt people to do strange things, such as move an entire town a mere mile and a half away. When collective fear turns into desperation, desperate people do even stranger things, such as blocking all attempts to expose the truth. The secret is always there to defend, but at what cost?

This particular mystery could be solved with the exhumation of the alien, as well as research and study of the pieces of the spaceship that were thrown into the well. Of course these activities are blocked and absolutely denied. Is this because they are no longer there, or is it because everyone is compelled to defend the secret? This prevents solving the mystery that has survived for over a century, although the answers may be glaringly obvious to some.

The following UFO accounts were discovered by Chad Lewis, author of *Hidden Headlines of Texas* and have been added to perhaps spark your interest and understanding of the events that took place in Aurora and surrounding towns during the late 1800s. As you read these actual newspaper accounts take note of the descriptions as they are remarkably similar to the way William Stanfield described Aurora in the early stages of its establishment. I believe that Stanfield had seen UFOs and possibly knew where a landing strip or UFO base was located. He knew the secret and he knew that Aurora would play a major part in the early communication and contact with UFOs. Does this base for UFOs exist even today? You be the judge.

From July 29, 1889 to May 3, 1909, there were numerous UFO stories related by prominent citizens who had witnessed them firsthand, as well as written accounts that appeared in newspapers across the state of Texas. Some of the articles mentioned the UFOs as a brilliant light in the sky, often being cigar shaped and over one hundred feet in length. They were described as being bright and luminous, while emitting green, purple, blue, orange, and red lights. Sounds included whirring, buzzing, and whizzing. Often thunderous sounds were cited. Account after account over the years describe UFOs with remarkably the same details; colored lights, sounds, and shapes.

In 1898 townsfolk from Garland, Texas, near Aurora, saw a UFO that descended, traveled slowly, and then suddenly changed its course and shot upward, throwing into the air three distinct bodies, each taking its own course and each being a different color; red, bright white, and blue. In 1908 in Denton, Texas, which is also near Aurora, an interesting account states that observers saw a UFO that shot upward and displayed small sections as they broke away from the parent body.

One particularly interesting account described a UFO that was witnessed by dozens of people in the skies over Brazos and Washington counties. The sky was illuminated with a smoky sulfur color. Various colors of violet, purple, and blue appeared, and then eerie script letters also appeared. The letters (M-M-T-U-W) were formed as the heavens became clear. Was this an obvious attempt at communication?

The following account is extremely interesting in that it reflects heavily on a similar account recorded in more recent times.

DALLAS MORNING NEWS
MAY 3, 1909 – * DUBLIN, TEXAS *

An airship passed over the city and the heavens were lit up as bright as day. A terrific explosion was heard from the unseen power.

PAST - FORWARD!

Now that you have read newspaper accounts of unidentified flying objects (UFOs) in the skies over Texas in the late 1800s, perhaps you would like to read a more recent and startling account of the same UFO phenomenon over the skies of Texas in 2008! I think you will find that some of the descriptions from the 1890s are very similar and in some cases identical to these today. How can people from another century describe an unidentified object exactly the same way? Because they saw exactly the same thing, in exactly the same area!

Here's a more recent article.

TEXARKANA GAZETTE

JANUARY 15, 2008 - STEPHENVILLE

* DUBLIN, TEXAS *

On January 8, 2008 the residents of the rural, sparsely settled town of Stephenville, Texas reported dozens of UFO sightings in and around Stephenville, Dublin, and Selden, Texas as well.

Several people including an airplane pilot, county constable, and several business owners reported seeing a large silent object with bright lights flying low and fast in the area. There were even some remarkable reports from three men who said they saw fighter jets chasing the unidentified object as it flew across the sky.

Steve Allen of Selden, Texas, a private airplane pilot, said that the unidentified object he saw was about a mile long and half a mile wide. He and two friends noticed it about 6:15 p.m. and determined that it was headed toward Stephenville. He added that "It was positively, absolutely nothing from these parts."

Local residents insist that whatever it was, it was much larger, quieter, faster, and was able to maneuver closer to the ground than an airplane. They stated that the unidentified object displayed lights that changed their configurations, which ruled out the possibility of them being attached to an airplane.

Ricky Sorrels of Dublin said that he saw a flat, metallic object hovering about three hundred feet over a pasture behind his house. He further stated that he has seen the unidentified object overhead on several occasions. He watched it through his rifle's telescope lens and described it as being very large and as having no appearance of seams, nuts, or bolts.

Maj. Karl Lewis, a spokesman for the 301st Fighter Wing at the Joint Reserve Naval Air Station in Fort Worth said that no F-16s or other aircraft from his base were in the air the night of January 8. He stated that the "object" in question may have been an illusion caused by two commercial airplanes.

Now how many of us believe this? You've only to re-read the above newspaper accounts for almost identical descriptions, albeit one hundred years apart, to see the similarity and grasp the truth of this reality.

Officials at the region's two Air Force Bases—Dyess in Abilene and Sheppard in Wichita Falls, Texas—also said that none of their aircraft were in the area during the week of January 8.

According to the Mutual UFO Network (Mufon), over two hundred UFO sightings are reported each month, mostly throughout California, Colorado, and Texas.

The more things change—the more they remain the same! Almost exactly one hundred years to the date of the previous newspaper accounts on May 3, 1909—a UFO was sighted over Dublin, Texas.

SEVEN
ENERGIZED
CEMETERIES

Ley lines of energy crisscross the earth forming magnificent invisible grid patterns. These lines help to channel the earth's energies from one sacred location to the next, creating a huge circuit board. Along these channels and at major intersections lie gateways and portals that allow spirit beings access to our realm. This sometimes allows unsuspecting ghost hunters a glimpse into alternate and parallel dimensions.

Cemeteries and graveyards that are established along these powerful ley lines quite naturally become supernatural spirit passageways—even more so when they are established at a site where the lines intersect.

These ley lines have been in existence since the beginning of time as we know it. Our ancestors and earlier cultures were well aware of them, and erected their standing stones, stone circles, burial mounds, pyramids, castles, cathedrals, sacred sites, churches, and cemeteries along these lines. These locations enhanced their worship and veneration of their gods and energized the departure of their loved ones to other realms of existence.

In 1921 an Englishman named Alfred Watkins had a sudden revelation that he referred to as "a flood of ancestral memory" (Watkins, 1925). While absorbed in scanning an old map of the Herefordshire countryside, he was astonished to see that various prehistoric sites such as standing stones, burial mounds, and cemeteries, all fell in straight lines with one another, even when those lines went directly through hills, over streams, and through fields, farmhouses, barns, and meadows. This so intrigued him that he began a lifelong search for the meaning of the lines.

From this amazing insight, combined with local and regional spirit-lore, he developed the theory of energy lines. He coined the term *ley lines* from the Saxon word for "cleared," which indicated that meadows and glades were cleared to define these lines or channels of the earth's energies. He surmised that these straight lines from one sacred site to another, although man-made, actually accessed the earth's basic energy grid. These direct lines could be located by dowsing the earth for an acceptable current, one which emitted positive energy.

By studying archaic landscapes, he was actually uncovering an entire occult history of the world, thereby leaving an amazing legacy for others to contemplate for years to come.

Our ancestors understood the magnetic energy associated with and emanating from these lines. Archaeological evidence supports the ancient practice of establishing these direct lines (sometimes called spirit paths) that has survived for centuries in Europe and America.

Ley lines are significant to ghost hunters because they link mysterious alignments and intersections of accumulated energy in churchyards, graveyards, and cemeteries around the country. In ancient Europe there seems to have been an intrinsic occult knowledge of ley lines and spirit roads that were used to carry the deceased to their final destinations.

These spiritual passageways spanned across the countryside, through fields, across rivers, over hills, and always in as straight a line as possible. Rural country folk even removed sections from stone walls and fences to accommodate these roads and ensure that they were as straight as possible.

These "corpse roads" and "spirit paths" were developed as people were forced to bury their dead away from their local parishes. Laws were enacted that forced them to bury their loved ones in the churchyard of the "Mother Church," which was usually located in the center of the surrounding parishes. It held all the burial rights and this created a great hardship for the people in outlying parishes. Because of this inconvenience they were forced to carry their deceased loved ones in walking funerals for long distances, and often over difficult terrains, but, always in a straight energized line to the cemetery. Dowsers were employed to create these roads and pathways; by using ancient techniques they were able to create with exactness a network of spirit pathways that followed positive energy lines, which of course would benefit the soul of the deceased as it journeyed to its final destination.

Although these lines had few physical demarcations, they were nevertheless very clear-cut geographical realities. As the practice endured, these corpse roads and spirit pathways were eventually marked with standing stones, stone altars, and sacred rocks. It is possible that these stones and altars were erected to define resting places for the pallbearers as well as the members of the funeral procession.

Despite all the confusing theories about ley lines, one thing remains clear. They do exist. They create direct lines to historically powerful locations, such as old fortresses, burial grounds, sacred sites, medieval castles, cathedrals, churches, and cemeteries. The flow of energy never stops.

There are slight variations with different countries and cultures, but the central idea of the deeply rooted spirit lore is that ghosts, spirits, doppelgangers, and who knows what else, move through the earth's spiritual landscape along these energized channels.

Over centuries spirit lore has developed from the practice of moving the deceased along these sometimes long and difficult ley lines. These lines have had many different names; corpse roads, spirit passageways, ghost lanes, and spirit ways, to name a few. Each country has it own variations—different, yet mysteriously the same.

Ghost lore tells us that a direct pathway close to the ground is the most effortless way for ghosts and spirits to travel. This is most often in a straight line, connecting places that were clear of any obstacles to avoid disturbing the spirits as they traveled back and forth.

There is also an abundance of folklore connected to ley lines, beginning with the most obvious: ghosts. The bodies of the deceased were carried along corpse roads to keep their spirits from returning to haunt the living—it was believed that if the dead were sufficiently energized they would complete their journey into the afterlife. There was also a widespread belief that if the deceased's feet were pointing away from their home, they would never return, so great care was taken to ensure that the body was facing the correct direction. Another ritual to prevent the spirit's return was to ensure that the route taken crossed bridges or stepping stones across small streams to prevent the ghost from returning, as ghosts were supposedly unable to cross running water.

Can you imagine for a moment what a funeral procession must have been like? People who are already grief-stricken and mourning were forced to travel across miles of complex countryside, across rivers and streams, in the heat or cold, and fearful all the while that if a ritual wasn't performed with exactness the dearly departed would return. In the event it was suspected that a spirit had returned home to the community where it had lived and died, elaborate mazes and labyrinths were often constructed to ensnare the wayward ghost or spirit.

It seems that almost all versions of spirit passageways and corpse roads go back to ancient cultures that had shamans, soothsayers, witch doctors, wise women, and Holy men. These seers were able to release their spirits from their bodies during trance states and could soar (supposedly) in straight lines to seek knowledge and inspiration. These flights of the soul have been experienced by seers of all cultures including Native Americans. Perhaps they are in part associated with all the bizarre phenomena that have been seen, heard, felt, and sensed along ley lines for centuries.

Many people have happened upon weird artifacts and unusual objects along these lines that could very possibly have been brought through portals. They have experienced luminous light spheres and odd configurations, ball lightning, orbs, and spook lights of all colors that move about in all directions.

Ley lines represent psychic energy and vortexes, whirlwinds and spinning shapes, all of which are seen with such consistency that they can't be ignored. One of the most mysterious and to some the most frightening are apparitions of men and women in full period dress. They have been seen walking up and down corpse roads and spirit paths, and of course in cemeteries across the country.

Extremely interesting to me are the fairy processions and nature spirits that have been sighted on the pathways. Having seen both fairies and elementals, I know that they exist. I would wager a bet that they establish their invisible communities near ley lines in order to access the positive energy found there.

Even more mysterious and startling are the sightings of UFOs and weird creatures either on the spirit passages or alongside them. Because they are also energy masses, they would of course be attracted to the energy in ley lines. Could the many appearances of reptilian creatures be due to these powerful energy lines? Do they possess knowledge of the earth's energy? Of course they do!

At the points where ley lines intersect, be it on a spirit path or in a cemetery there will be a vortex of accumulated energy. This is where luminous portals and vortexes will occur. This allows beings from other dimensions to enter our spiritual atmosphere and gain access to our realm of existence.

Perhaps a word of warning is needed here, especially for ghost hunters who will be wandering around in dark unknown territories. Areas such as cemeteries, abandoned and isolated areas, and especially places that were once government installations may prove very dangerous to the uninformed. Remember to always expect the unexpected, because you never know who or what will appear at these power points or worse yet, what you might very subtly be led into.

Better to be aware than end up in another dimension. Yes, I am serious!

Energy currents are emitted from the earth at different intervals and in varying degrees of intensity. Ghosts and unearthly creatures may appear only at times when conditions of the current are optimized and they can draw on this energy for their own personal agendas.

It was inevitable that a form of divination would develop associated with ley lines. In ancient Europe on Halloween and Midsummer's Eve, a community seer would hold a midnight vigil at the entrance to a cemetery, on a corpse road, or at the intersection of a spirit passageway, in order to divine the future of the people in his village or community. He would wait patiently for a clairvoyant vision regarding who would die in the coming year. Apparently the doppelganger of the soon-to-be deceased would appear to the seer. They would pass down the corpse road, enter the cemetery, and disappear into the darkness. If a vision of the dying person or persons was not forthcoming, the same information could be gleaned through clairaudience, and the seer would hear the name or names of the person who would die in the upcoming year. We have no knowledge of how these insights and information were received by the community or what rituals or preparations were made to comfort the potentially disembodied country folk.

There are two kinds of ley lines. Although historically and traditionally ley lines are straight and narrow, there are also leys that are spiral in configuration and the energy flows in a circular motion, as opposed to a straight pathway of energy.

The energy in the center of the spiral or circle would without a doubt be the strongest as it accumulated in the center and would be diminished toward the outward edges (www.flickr.com). It's very possible that these spirals of whirling energy occur where ley lines intersect, and I suspect that they also occur at the entrances of castles, cathedrals, cemeteries, as well as caves and tunnels. This would be interesting research in and of itself.

If ley lines create energized spirit passageways, and I believe that they do, then cemeteries are undoubtedly mystical force fields—especially if they are circular in design.

It is no coincidence that cemeteries are haunted; however, it may not always be due to disembodied spirits. When ley lines are applied there are almost unlimited possibilities in what is seen, heard, felt, and sensed inside churchyards, cemeteries, and graveyards. This is where ghost hunters would no doubt be challenged to uncover, define, and document eerie phenomena.

CIRCULAR BURIALS

Traditionally, churches and cemeteries are square or rectangular in design. However, there exists today in various locations across Europe and in the United States as well, circular cemeteries and circular burial plots within traditional cemeteries. These often overlooked and unusual burial sites could be centers of activity. Due to their formation, location on ley lines, or at ley intersections, one would naturally experience the amazing phenomena associated with ley lines.

Circular burials are not new—they have been around for centuries. I believe that in ancient times every burial site was probably dowsed for positive energy before the first burial ever took place. These circular burials are evidenced in Europe as burial mounds, as well as in smaller parish cemeteries. In America, they were established by various Native American tribes and created in cemeteries by prominent citizens of newly formed colonial townships.

Such cemeteries are still in existence today in the towns of Pittsfield, Massachusetts; Chicago, Illinois; Mobile, Alabama; Erie, Pennsylvania; and Charleston, South Carolina, to name a few. In Pittsfield, a central monument was erected and members of the family were buried like spokes of a wheel emanating from the hub or center. Affluent citizens would purchase the center plot in a prestigious area of the cemetery and place family and extended family members in a circle around them. Considering that the energy is strongest in the middle, how would it affect the disembodied spirit connected to that particular body? What if it became super-energized?

There is a fascinating Druid burial plot in the Waldheim Cemetery in Chicago, Illinois. Waldheim Cemetery was established in 1873 as a non-religious cemetery where Freemasons, Gypsies, and Druids, as well as immigrants to Chicago could be laid to rest without regard to religious affiliation (www.flickr .com). Standing ceremoniously within its boundaries is an amazingly tall, magnificent Druid monument. The outstanding medieval octagonal-shaped granite pedestal has a statue of an impressive Druid priest on top. He boasts an awesome presence, appearing shrouded in mystery as he holds court over the cemetery. He has a long beard, and stands next to an altar of standing stones. He is holding an unusual staff with the head of a child on top. His astounding height and design are amazing examples of expert craftsmanship. There can be little doubt as to the possibility of him stepping down from his lofty home to walk among the graves, especially since he is in the center of the circular leys designed for him.

Around the base are three concentric circles of stone curbing carved to resemble logs, with radial spokes of similar design. This monument was erected in 1881 and contains many of the symbols associated with the Druid Order, including the All-Seeing Eye within a triangle. In 1883 Chicago was home to sixteen local Druid lodges, called "Groves." The Druids revere Merlin as a saint and follow "The Seven Precepts of Merlin." Once again one has to wonder how this circular burial plot affects the spirits of the deceased as well as mourners and visitors to the cemetery.

In Mobile, Alabama, the 150-acre, old Catholic Church Cemetery was established with a very unique circular design. In 1828 Archbishop Michael Portier chose a site for the cemetery and had the grounds designed in a large circle with the grave plots pointed toward the center. It was no easy task to lay out a precise circle on uneven ground and was certainly a challenge for the surveyor. However upon its completion there were three concentric rings instead of the traditional east/west configurations of most cemeteries. At the center of the circle is a magnificent marble monument dedicated to the Daughters of Charity. As the older part of the cemetery filled, a new section was designed. An interesting aspect of the newer section is that it was laid out at the Archbishop's request in a grid configuration. Obviously Archbishop Portier had occult knowledge of ley lines. Without a doubt he either dowsed the area himself or had someone do it for him, in order to access the powerful ley lines of energy.

My approach to ley lines and spirit passageways may not be scientific, but I am clairvoyant, and this book was not written for scientists or skeptics.

You may think that ley lines are just lines with no significance, or pure fantasy, or nothing at all, but my own clairvoyant experiences validate my perception of how the earth's energies are distributed around the world, manifested in cemeteries, and used for healing in our society today.

I also believe that ley lines should be considered in reference to the migratory routes of birds and animals. I believe they can detect the magnetic energy in ley lines and that it enables them to navigate back and forth, much the same as ghosts or beings from other planets and dimensions.

There will always be questions, and perhaps the answer will come through the exploration of quantum physics, but until then the scientific proof that so many people seem to need so badly may be just out of reach, in the realm of spirit.

I believe we shouldn't discount or ignore occult forms of knowledge that have stood the tests of time just because they seems foreign to us or we don't readily understand them. It is possible that it may be just the information we need to energize our souls and spiral us to higher spiritual acceptance.

EIGHT
CEMETERY STATUARY

As a paranormal investigator I have found that people are either attracted to, or repelled by, lifelike statues of people or angels in cemeteries. I am very attracted to them. What intrigues me the most about statuary and always catches my attention are the beautiful details in stone of their clothing, hair, and their eyes, especially if they look too real.

When I first began to write about haunted cemeteries, and statuary in particular, I recalled a myth I had heard. I want to share it with you as an introduction to the beautifully sculptured, energized statues we see in cemeteries today. Victor Hugo noted this expression of energy in its most magnificent form, observing: "To the sculptor form is everything, and nothing. It is nothing without the spirit!"

The ancient Greek myth of Pygmalion and Galatea is an interesting story that symbolizes the connection of vibrational energies and divine spiritual intervention, as well as paranormal communications (Morford,2009; Hazel, 2002).

Pygmalion, King of Cypress, decided to create his own ideal companion. Being an expert sculptor, with great skill he chiseled a female statue from the finest ivory. His work was of such perfection that she seemed to be alive. Pygmalion admired his creation and ultimately fell in love with it. He dressed the statue in gowns of rare beauty. He placed a ring on her finger and a necklace of pearls about her neck.

Pygmalion was anxious for the festival of Aphrodite to arrive. It was celebrated with great ceremonial splendor throughout Greece, and Pygmalion had a special reason for attending the festival—to profess his devotion to the gods, and to make a timid request to the goddess Aphrodite. "Please give me my statue for my wife." Aphrodite, being present and knowing his inner thoughts, granted Pygmalion his heart's desire as a token of her favor.

Upon returning home he noticed that his ivory statue seemed lovelier than ever. With great reverence he placed a kiss upon her lips and was astonished that she appeared warm to his caress. As he stood filled with wonder and happiness his statue moved. She embodied all the grace and charm with which he had envisioned her. Pygmalion, in his desire to create an ethereal essence, had imbued vibrational energy into his heart's desire. Indeed she was *alive*.

As we wander around in cemeteries, perhaps lost in thought or grief, sometimes seclusion and silence engulf us and for a moment, or possibly even for hours, we become one with the universe. The poignancy of nostalgia added to our emotions may propel us into an infinite realm of surreal communication with unseen entities, ghosts, magnificent celestial statues, and deeply moving soul effigies.

Have you ever walked through an isolated graveyard as the moon's light cascades over seemingly life-like marble angels? These beautiful statues seem to come alive as time and space cease to exist in the silence that envelopes them. Some may have their heads lowered in reverence, while others may seem to be stepping down from their stone pedestals.

Do their eyes seem to follow you as you walk casually in and out of their view? As moonlight shimmers around them do they appear to be embodied with an ethereal energy bringing them to life? If you are ever alone in a cemetery late at night, you may see things, hear things, and sense things that reach far beyond your normal perception of the world we live in.

Perhaps you will hear someone whisper your name as you pass by. Do you sense that they can read your thoughts as you gaze at them in wonder? Or maybe you've felt a tug at your heart strings upon seeing small winged cherubs rousing from sleep in their marble cradles. If you have experienced these feelings you are not alone—there are stone angels watching you and perhaps ghosts wanting to communicate with you as you heighten your awareness of other dimensions.

What will the angelic faces of the stone angels convey? Their expressions may very well mirror your own thoughts and feelings as they increase your understanding of death and other realms of existence. Listen to the silence with an open heart. Can you hear what the statues are saying? Can you sense their messages of spiritual indulgence?

You may hear someone call out your name as you walk past, in an attempt to get you to listen and respond to your own soul's mysterious voice. As night deepens and misty fog creeps softly around you, the statues may become celestial messengers with stories and spiritual truths to share. They may also have secrets to tell or they may encourage you to do something to soothe someone's soul.

How is all of this possible? Our lives are filled with distractions, noise, and a constant bombardment of high frequency vibrations. Silence is the key to understanding the dimension we live in. We cannot be open and receptive to spiritual communications and visitations when we are distracted. Spiritual beings contact us through our hearts, souls, and emotions.

If statues are indeed alive, imbued with energy, and I believe that they are, one has to wonder how this can be true. For the answer to this question we must turn to the sculptor who created it, the person who requisitioned it, and ultimately to its intended recipient.

I have a genuine admiration for the creativity and sensitivity of the stonecutters, sculptors, and engravers from the past. They created angels and picturesque statuary in all forms and sizes, exceptional in their stylized and sometimes perfect likenesses of the deceased. They captured a personality as well as bringing a soul's essence alive. Their significance however goes far beyond being elaborate decorations. They created a remembrance erected to watch over or accompany departed souls on their journeys into another dimension.

Celestial angels, cheerful cherubs, and lifelike statuary were often created for mass production and because of this many are similar. However, many sculptors were called upon to create something unique and unusual and their meticulously created and delicately carved statues are alive with energy even today. This energy plays a definite role in the magnificent statuary that has survived centuries of nature's wrath and man's neglect.

Everything that exists in the universe is ultimately pure energy, and that energy encompasses a vibrational frequency that includes every thought we think, every word we speak, every emotion we feel, and every action we take. Everything that exists, everything we hear, see, feel, taste, and experience is energy in one form or another. This energy can be absorbed and contacted. It is a very subtle force, and it has memory and consciousness, whether we acknowledge it or not.

It is easy for us to see how living things are filled with energy and are vibrating at various frequencies just as we are. Both animate and inanimate objects also have energy fields and the same universal principals of energy apply to both.

So how, or more importantly, why, do we differentiate between the two? What is keeping us from accepting the truth about energy and how it connects, interacts, and is without a doubt the very core of our existence?

Perhaps we need to relate to energy as children do. They don't try to distinguish between living and inanimate objects. They simply accept energy in whatever form it presents itself. Have we ever been able to discern what is real and what is not?

Native Americans believed that everything has a soul. I believe this too. I also believe that every craftsman, in fact everyone who transforms energy into a new form, knows that he is tapping into transcendental truths. He knows that his work is a representation of what is seen beyond the veil of illusion. And this has never been more obvious than when one gazes upon celestial angels or magnificent statuary.

Beautiful, antiquated, winged angels are an excellent example of how sculptors imbue their statues with energy. Male and female angels are portrayed with powerful wings that convey the materialization of ethereal energy, giving flight to the energy within. Their appearance in graveyards and cemeteries is a manifestation of that energy.

Although they were created to be valued and appreciated, the visual sensations statues produce are often mixed in the observer's perception, especially when all the senses come into play. Their strange, enigmatic beauty gives them personal identities and unique personalities. Whether visualized and created as angels or statues with effeminate qualities, they are usually attired in flowing gowns or robes. If you were to touch their celestial garments you would probably feel the warmth that permeates and magnifies their spiritual essence. You would feel energy that celebrates life and encompasses the frequency of death. In many instances they may be waiting patiently, anticipating your visit. They are waiting to bequeath to you a legacy of universal knowledge.

Inasmuch as statues symbolize the mysteries of the universe through their relationship with the space they inhabit, they also remain steadfast reminders that there is no death and we do not die. They are telling us that it is not death that is being mourned, but the sometimes unacceptable, yet temporary separation from our loved ones.

People from all walks of life, all cultures, including ghost hunters, have had eerie, uncomfortable, and sometimes just plain weird experiences with statues in cemeteries. For centuries souls hidden in the simplicity and splendor of statuary have been seen moving about, turning on their pedestals, disappearing and reappearing, walking through the cemetery and otherwise joining the ranks of the living on occasion.

After a statue has been created to represent a deceased individual it sometimes becomes a doppelganger in a sense. Look for facial expressions that change appearance, a smile or a frown, as well as eyes that follow your every move. This alone can be very disconcerting, especially if you are standing close enough to hear a heartbeat! Cemeteries and graveyards are spiritual dimensions of unseen power and the statues residing there, whether archaic or contemporary, have access to that energy.

The following stories represent how energy interacts with animate and inanimate objects. From magnificent marble angels to lifelike statues, you will see how easily energy can be seen, heard, and felt as it brings soul effigies to life.

I will begin with my own personal encounter with one such majestic male angel. As a powerful example of a celestial messenger, he helped to awaken my sense of universal connectedness. He showed me that energy is eternal and interwoven as it interacts with one unique form after another, all different yet basically the same. He helped me realize that I could ignore and look beyond the boundaries of time and space as I knew them. I am ever grateful for our meeting and his presence in my life.

My day began with the usual routine of getting my husband off to work and the children ready for school. As soon as I put them on the bus, I grabbed my purse and shopping list and headed into town at breakneck speed. I was fuming internally over the fact that there were never enough hours in the day, *never enough time.*

The tension within my soul seemed to rise with each new errand I ran. There was no joy to be found in rushing to and fro like a mad woman in a whirlwind.

I reviewed my day on the way home and found that I was tired, frustrated, and agitated. Why? Hadn't I accomplished all that I had set out to do and more? Hadn't I convinced myself that I was the perfect shopper, mother, and wife? Didn't I act like a saint when a man cut me off in traffic, almost causing an accident? Wasn't I sweet when I didn't scream at the young sales clerk who couldn't add, count, or think for that matter? Hadn't I proven beyond a shadow of a doubt just how perfect I was? Suddenly, I realized that I had veered off my usual route home and was on a country road headed in a direction I had never been before.

I stopped the car in the middle of the road to get my bearings, when out of my peripheral vision I sensed movement. I turned to see the most incredible angel I have ever seen. He was waiting on the top of a gigantic monument as if holding his own private court while seated on his throne of marble. He rose stately among the clouds as he reigned over a long-forgotten graveyard.

The graveyard was almost concealed by huge trees and dense underbrush. Beautiful silver-leaf maple trees sparkled and gave the late afternoon light a celestial aura. I trembled as I pulled the car to the side of the road. For a mere second, fleeting thoughts of butter, ice cream, and other things in my shopping bags that would melt entered my mind. However, one more glance in the angel's direction banished all images of day-to-day reality from my mind.

As I gently lifted the handle on the old rusted wrought-iron gate of the graveyard, I felt my hands begin to tingle. I know I probably jumped a foot high when the gate creaked and slammed shut behind me. Somehow I managed to take a few more steps forward. Suddenly, I felt as if I was walking on air. I seemed to glide ever so quietly into the angel's domain.

As I stood there mesmerized by his commanding presence, I heard him whisper my name. His gentle voice in my ear was soothing to my soul. I was filled with peace and contentment as all the tensions of the day, all the fears from the past, and the chaos of my life seemed to flow downward into the soft earth beneath my feet.

I don't know how long I had been standing there when a brisk breeze broke my reverie and I realized that evening shadows had settled around me. The radiant light of day had been replaced by a soft, luminous darkness. However, I felt safe and secure as I gazed into his eyes. As I turned to leave I searched for the name on the tombstone. There was none; only these words: *"There was never enough time."*

I trembled as I stood there with tears streaming down my face. I promised to always remember this obvious message. This experience has added validity to my perception of unseen energies, inanimate entities, and spiritual communication.

The following cemetery mysteries include an angel that turns on its pedestal at night, an illustrious WWII soldier, and a mysterious mermaid statue. Some may be complete myths, urban legends, or merely folklore. Some are without question true, however weird the phenomenon surrounding them may seem. Some were easy to verify, while others may forever remain a mystery. Some I have personally witnessed and it was an exciting event. Others I have investigated and didn't see them move or create any paranormal activity. However, they are no less intriguing, and just because I didn't see it, doesn't necessarily mean that it didn't happen.

THE TURNING ANGEL

For over two hundred years foreigners as well as Americans have been buried in the one-hundred-acre Natchez City Cemetery. Extraordinary citizens from the south, military heroes, and hundreds of others share their final resting places in this magnificent cemetery.

This cemetery was established in 1822 when the remains were moved from the old burial grounds in Memorial Park to the present location, on a high bluff above the Mississippi River. It evolved and grew into a beautiful outdoor archive of Mississippi legend and folklore, as well as a final resting place for the famous and infamous. Beautiful statuary and elaborate tombstones, some inscribed with romantic and mysterious messages, seem to draw portraits of mystifying characters.

As a paranormal investigator, every cemetery I've seen where disinterred bodies were re-buried has been mysteriously haunted by ghosts and unusual light anomalies. The Natchez Cemetery is no exception.

The site that was originally green fields and hills overlooking the Mississippi River has been shaped into a garden-like park with grassy plots surrounded by towering oak and cypress trees draped in Spanish moss. Beautiful dogwoods, magnolias, and camellia bushes blend in with rows of azaleas, and scattered antique roses framed by lanes of crêpe myrtles.

This cemetery offers an unusual setting for many unique art forms. From lifelike marble statues, imposing mausoleums, and graceful monuments to exquisite tombstones engraved with delicate flower designs and Spenserian script, these art forms create a celestial view of reverent dimensions beyond our own. However, after dark the cemetery takes on a different persona. The night comes alive with sounds and noises—some explainable, others not. The elaborately fenced-in plots blend in with the darkness as if to encapsulate their disembodied souls.

In the month of March in 1908, there was an enormous explosion at the Natchez Drug Company. The blast was so intense that it totally destroyed the five-story building that housed the company, killing many people, including the employees working there at the time. The explosion put the drug company out of business. The owner of the company was so devastated that he purchased a lot in which to bury his employees and he also purchased a magnificent angel monument to place at their gravesites. This beautiful monument now overlooks five headstones, each bearing the same date of death.

Towering regally over the silent tombstones is a magnificent Turning Angel. This awesome image gently peruses the book of life she holds in her hands. She is both graceful and pensive as she gently turns to cast a shadow on the resting souls below.

She has been seen by many visitors as she turns around on her pedestal as if to follow them as they stroll through the cemetery. She appears to follow light and movement as well. And people driving by late at night have seen her move. How intriguing. Maybe she wishes she could come down from her lofty pedestal and visit the world below. Perhaps she does.

> *Though upon your lofty throne you are found,*
> *Whose footprints are those upon the ground?*

WWI SOLDIER

Rose Hill Cemetery was established in 1874 as the town of Texarkana, Texas began to grow in population. There are over seventy Confederate soldiers and three unidentified Union soldiers buried there.

Not all cemeteries are haunted in the traditional sense of the word; however this is one particular cemetery that seems to be paranormally active during the day as well as at night. It is full of ghosts and because of this it has become one of my favorite haunts. I go there often with friends, family, and fellow ghost hunters. Rose Hill Cemetery is located in an older part of town secluded behind factories and abandoned buildings that create an ominous atmosphere.

One has to cross railroad tracks to enter the cemetery gates. There is a long-standing legend that if you are caught in the cemetery at night as a train passes by you will never be able to leave, dead or alive. The cemetery's very location makes it even weirder at night and potentially dangerous as well. Local police have advised us to stay away because as they put it, "We have found more bodies on top of the ground in that cemetery than there are buried below."

I am particularity fascinated by the huge memorial statue of a WWI soldier at the very back of the cemetery. It stands as a tribute to his bravery. I never go there without being overcome with emotion and I am not entirely sure that it is *my* emotions I am experiencing. I know several people who have experienced the same thing while visiting the gravesite of Corporal Otis Henry. Perhaps we were feeling his mother's pain and grief. She obviously felt these emotions very deeply to erect such a magnificent monument.

Corporal Otis Henry was gassed near Vincey, France and died on October 6, 1918 while serving with the 359th Infantry Division of the American Expeditionary Forces stationed in France. He was buried in the Rose Hill Cemetery three years later, on June 29, 1921.

This elaborate monument consists of not one but four lifesize statues. The first and most prominent soul effigy can be seen from the cemetery entrance. It is a life-size statue of a WWI soldier, arm raised as if ready to toss the grenade he holds in his hand. He is sculpted in his full Army uniform with exacting details. He stands erect and tall atop a ten-foot pedestal reaching into the sky overhead. The second statue of him is a six-foot likeness of him before he left for the war. He is attired in a business suit.

Next to him stands a seven-foot- tall angel. She is wearing a celestial gown of starry elegance and has a look of pride and motherly devotion on her face. On his left is a smaller angel, just as impressive and serene. Both angels seem to indicate by their very presence their ability to communicate between the realm of spirit and the world of mortal reality.

Otis Henry's soul effigy is spectacular. Gazing up at him one will come away with a deep sense of patriotism. Legend has it that "If you go to see Otis, he will come to see you." There are numerous reports of people who have awakened at night to see him standing at the foot of their beds. Once you have gazed into his eyes it's almost impossible to remove him from your memory.

He stands today in a very ornate, six-foot Victorian iron-fenced enclosure. It remains locked, perhaps to protect him as he gave his life to protect others. Some people have seen him as he steps down from his lofty pedestal at night to walk among the rows of identical white WWII markers in the cemetery. He was seen quite unexpectedly late one night by one of our investigators as he strolled in front of his gravesite. He appeared to be surrounded by an aura of rainbow colors. Orb activity always accompanies him and encompasses his gravesite—large ones, small ones, and clusters as well. This is truly a sight to behold on a moonlit night, especially if you are lucky enough to make contact with him.

One of our team members took an awesome photograph of Otis in the early morning hours of an investigation. It appears in the picture that he is actually beside himself as if to duplicate and magnify his presence. He stands in his place of honor as a protective guardian over those who have died in battle.

Remember, if you go to see Otis, Otis will come to see you!

MERMAID STATUE

What could be more mysterious than a grave with a funerary statue of a Mermaid gracing the gravesite? Not too much I would think! However, mysterious she is, and a mystery she is destined to remain, possibly forever.

The statue was found on the island of Manara, off the west coast of Scotland. She was later moved to the Louvre in Paris, France where she now resides. This mysterious mermaid statue is listed as the "Siren on Funerary Monument, Number 33," at the Louvre.

However, she lacks the traditional tail of a mermaid. Instead she has legs and feet that appear to be covered in scales. Does she represent a mermaid, a mythological siren, or could she actually represent something altogether different? Could this be the reason she was moved from her island paradise and secreted away in the confines of the Louvre? Could she actually represent a reptilian being?

Burials of mer-people were not unusual during the seventeenth and eighteenth centuries. They were seen quite frequently and were well documented by everyone from the captains, crews, and fishermen of huge ships, Christopher Columbus, and even the priests of the day.

One such sighting and resultant burial took place at the Mermaid's Grove near Nunton Benbeculla. This particular mermaid is rumored to be buried in the sands in the area around Nuton. In 1830 some peasant women who were gathering seaweed spotted a mermaid in the water close to the shore. They tried in vain to catch her, but she was too clever for them. Then a young boy startled her by throwing stones in her direction. Evidently she was hit and she disappeared below the water and away from view. A few days after the sighting the tiny body of the mermaid washed ashore on the beach.

She was described as having the upper body of a young girl and the lower half of a salmon without scales. She was buried with a shawl in a small, specially made coffin, somewhere along the highest tide mark.

Funerary art and cemetery statuary will forever remain either hauntingly beautiful or frightening to mourners and visitors alike. Every craftsman or sculptor expressed themselves through their creations and in so doing imbued them with energy. As a result many magnificent statues, angels, and soul effigies have gained a reputation of being alive or at the very least haunted, and rightly so!

NINE
CEMETERY
TOMBSTONES

For centuries men and women have expressed a desire for immortality and in their need to be remembered they have created unique and intriguing tombstones. These markers are often inscribed with spiritual, inspirational, cryptic, or sometimes just plain weird messages for everyone to see.

Every gravestone or tombstone is a testament to the fact that someone lived and died. There are millions of interesting tombstones engraved with names, dates, symbols, and images that convey obvious and sometimes mysterious messages for future generations. Ghost hunters in urban cemeteries and isolated graveyards often stumble upon revealing tombstones which add to the mystery and mystique of an investigation, especially when there is paranormal activity attached to the gravesite. Although it is easy to understand why people place loving tributes as memorials for their friends and loved ones, it is not always so easy to understand why they would choose to immortalize death with occult sayings or cryptic messages.

Cemeteries are the final resting places for millions of famous and infamous individuals who have helped to shape our country and perhaps alter history in one way or another. The following stories represent how these people often leave lasting impressions on society. How they wish to be remembered, or not, is often displayed as a cryptic work of art, to say nothing of the mysteries they leave behind.

LILLY GRAY
VICTIM OF THE BEAST – 666

If a visit to the Statue of Liberty is the recommended introduction to New York City, then a visit to the cemetery on the mountainside at 4th and N Street is a good starting point for Salt Lake City, Utah. The cemetery encompasses over 250 acres and contains at least nine miles of roadways. As if this is not enough to make it interesting; a gravesite in the cemetery holds an intriguing mystery in the form of one of the most unusual epitaphs I have ever read.

In a serene section of the sprawling cemetery grounds is a traditional marble marker. However, the epitaph engraved on it is anything but traditional. It bears a mystifying message for everyone to see. It very subtly conjures up images of the devil, hellfire and brimstone, and the Mark of the Beast. It raises dark, cryptic images that encourage visitors to speculate about the life of the woman who is buried there. It has aroused fear and curiosity, and has manifested rumor after rumor. It ignites the imagination and touches the soul, sending goose bumps up and down the spine.

The spine-tingling epitaph reads:

Lilly Gray

Born: June 6, 1881

Died: Nov. 14, 1958

"Victim of the Beast – 666"

Lilly's marker lies among surrounding headstones that are inscribed with loving memorials and endearments to family members.

"Victim of the Beast" is a highly stimulating phrase that refers to the New Testament book of Revelations, in which chapter 13 has been interpreted to refer to the Antichrist. The burning question on the minds of everyone who sees her mysterious marker is without a doubt, "What does it mean?"

followed by a continuous stream of questions such as: "How was she a victim of the Beast?" And "Who was the Beast?" These questions are as unnerving as the epitaph itself. How can Lilly rest in eternal peace with such an inscription hovering above her?

These questions and more have increased the mystery surrounding Lilly Gray for fifty years. No one seems to know what it means. The headstone was set in 1958 and additional mysteries cloak the marker itself. For example, the engraving on the marker is inaccurate. There are also several discrepancies between the information on the gravestone and the information held in public records.

Her birthdate is actually recorded as June 4, 1880 and not June 6, 1881 as inscribed on her marker. It also appears that her first name, Lilly, was misspelled, as Lily with one "L" is the correct spelling. Could these errors be an engraver's mistake, or a deliberate act to change the vibration of her name? Could this apply to her birth date as well?

The following is an excerpt of her obituary that appeared in the *Salt Lake Tribune* on November 15, 1958:

Mrs. Lily Edith Gray, 78, 1216 Pacific Ave. Died Friday, 11:10 a.m. in a Salt Lake Hospital of natural causes. Born June 4, 1880 in Canada. Salt Lake City resident since 1950. Married to Elmer Lewis Gray, July 10, 1952 at Elko, Nevada. Survivors, husband and several nieces and nephews.

Many clues and assumptions have emerged over the years regarding her mysterious epitaph; some that stretch the imagination. From numerology, to an association with the sinister

Aleister Crowley or views of the beast as money or an illness, to the infamous Route 666 in southern Utah.

Further clues to the mystery may be found in the decorative floral engraving on the headstone. The flower on Lily's gravestone is the evening primrose. Although its traditional meaning is peace and life everlasting, it also has a seemingly darker symbolic meaning indicated by the flower's nickname, "Devil's Lantern." Could someone have been aware of this secondary meaning and thereby had it etched in stone to add to the mysterious, cryptic message?

The investigation into the meaning behind Lily Gray's mysterious epitaph is far from over. Richelle Hawks, a longtime resident of Salt Lake City, has recorded extensive research into the mysterious inscription and its enigmatic meaning. A visit to her websites and the following associated content site will reveal much of her research: (www.associatedcontent.com /article/1784322).

She was led to research Lily's husband Elmer Gray, who died on Halloween in 1964 and is buried in the same cemetery, yet some distance from his wife. She found that he had an extensive criminal background and concluded from reading documents related to his pardons appeals that he was probably very frustrated and disillusioned with his life. He was also very vocal about government conspiracies and supposed personal victimization.

Given this information, Richelle surmised that it is highly probable that Elmer was the person responsible for placing the enigmatic phrase "Victim of the Beast, 666" on his wife's gravestone. As he may have been Lily's closest surviving relative he was probably the one who made all the funeral arrangements.

Research on this mysterious gravestone has proven to be a maze of dead-end twists and turns. There is obviously a lack of information to support just about any theory put forth for consideration. The only tangible information is her obvious gravestone marker and her obituary.

Lily's legendary marker will no doubt remain a riddle for years to come. With so many questions, and so few answers, she will forever remain a mystery.

CARIBBEAN ISLAND— MYSTERY TOMBSTONE

To the tourists who visit Tobago it may at first be just another exciting Caribbean destination; an island that once thrived on sugar plantations and is said to have been the island that the fabled Robinson Crusoe discovered. However, there is much more to Tobago than legend and folklore.

Tobago is a small island located in the Caribbean Sea. In 1498 Columbus claimed the island for Spain. However, because the Carib Indians who inhabited the island were so aggressive and warlike, they prevented colonization of the island until late into the seventeenth century. Over the next two centuries, the natives were taken into slavery by the Spaniards and exposed to hard labor and European plagues that virtually wiped out the entire population.

Tobago's history was very volatile. After the Spaniards defeated the Caribs, the English, French, Dutch, and various bands of pirates made attempts at dominating the island. This colony of Spain developed slowly, attracting the Catalan Capuchin missionaries. During the Napoleonic Wars, in 1797, the British seized the opportunity to take the island from the Spaniards and in 1825, Tobago came under British rule.

The seaside village of Plymouth, settled by the Dutch in 1633, holds one of the island's strangest mysteries. In the southwestern part of Tobago a grave marks the final resting place of a twenty-three-year-old woman named Betty Stivens, and her baby. Both died in 1783. The tombstone at this gravesite carries an unusual inscription that has puzzled generations of locals and many visitors to the island. Distinct cultures and faiths are blended amid the rhythmic beat of Calypso music, lush rainforest, white sands, and magnificent waterfalls to provide the backdrop for this enigmatic island mystery (www.trinicenter.com/Tobago, and www.Tobagotoday.com).

Here is the inscription:

Within these walls are deposited the bodies of Mrs. Betty Stiven and her child. She was the beloved wife of Alex. B. Stiven. To the end of his days [he] will deplore her death which happened upon the 25th of November in 1783 in the 23rd year of her age. What was remarkable of her, she was a mother without knowing it, and a wife without letting her husband know it, except by her kind indulgence to him.

Who was Betty Stiven? How did she die? What story does the inscription tell? Research reveals that antiquated records in the archives of the Anglican Church in Scarborough show an old register of baptisms, marriages, and deaths dated 1781–

1817. On page two of this old volume is listed the following information:

Three mulatto children of Alexander Stiven, one son
by the name of Alexander and two daughters, one by
the name of Sally and the other named Mary.

There is however no record of a marriage for Betty Stiven. Betty Stiven was an African woman and Alexander Stiven was a wealthy slave master who is reported to have paid to become warden for the area. Betty was not the woman's real name as she was African, but was instead a pet name meaning "darling" that was bestowed by a white man with amorous feeling for a woman.

Wealthy Alexander Stiven was noted as having a secret relationship with Betty that began when she was twelve years old. It would not have been considered proper in those days to make public any liaison with a slave, but Stiven had a special fondness for this young woman.

Betty bore her master's children, but during her pregnancy she became very ill and was confined to bed. On September 25, 1783, while in an unconscious state, she gave birth to quadruplets. One died but three others survived—a son, and two daughters.

The children were hastily given away to other female slaves who were sworn to secrecy and who also pretended to have been raped to explain the presence of the babies. This allowed Stiven to conceal his intimate relationship with Betty. When she regained consciousness she was not aware that she had given birth to three children and was also unable to prove that she had a relationship with Alexander Stiven.

Betty was considered to be his wife. Customs during that day and time dictated that as long as a man was responsible for a woman's loss of virginity she automatically became his wife and they were considered to be married.

Solemnization before a minister of religion or someone with authority to perform marriages was not considered necessary. Betty was Stiven's wife, but not having gone to the altar or taken part in any other ritual she was not aware that for all intents and purposes she was his wife.

Unable to recover from her illness Betty died on November 25, 1783 at the age of twenty-three, not knowing that she had become a mother.

So fond was Alexander of Betty that he followed a traditional ritual of the times and placed 800 pounds of gold and three puncheons of rum in her tomb. Betty was buried next to his house. It is said that Alexander wrote the words that are now inscribed on Betty's tomb in such a way that he alone could understand, but would be a mystery to others. It was necessary in those days to conceal interracial relationships because of the stigma attached.

Although she never recovered to raise her children and live a full life, she will always remain as mysterious as the island paradise where she is buried.

PUZZLE TOMBSTONES

Rushes Cemetery near Crosshill, Wellesley Township, Ontario, contains two very unique and unusual tombstones (Lamb, 1992; Brown, 2007). Although rarely seen in today's society, puzzle tombstones existed during the mid to late 1800s. The puzzle tombstones in Rushes Cemetery mark the gravesite of two women; Henrietta and Susanna Bean, who were the wives of Samuel Bean.

Samuel Bean was at one time a teacher, who later became a doctor and eventually a pastor in the Evangelical Association. While practicing as a physician he lived in Linwood, Ontario and it was during this time period that he erected the puzzle tombstones for his first two wives. He later married for a third time and lived in New York, but was reportedly lost at sea off the coast of Cuba in 1904.

Henrietta and Susanna Bean were the first two wives of Samuel. Henrietta Fury, Samuel's first wife, was born in Philadelphia in 1842 and married Samuel Bean there early in 1865 at the age of twenty-three. She died on September 27, 1865 after only seven months of marriage. Her funeral card was a puzzle with nineteen letters across and nineteen letters down. Samuel Bean was clearly a brilliant man with a searching mind who found pleasure in creating conundrums. The reader started with the middle letter and read outward in a spiral. The card read:

In memoriam, Henrietta Fury Bean, born in Pennsylvania, married in Philadelphia to Samuel Bean, M.D. and went with him to Canada, leaving all her friends behind. Died in Linwood the 27th of September 1865 after an illness of 11 weeks, aged 23 years, 2 months, and 17 days, she was a model wife—1 of 100—much regretted by her sorrowing husband and all who knew her—lived a godly life for 5 years and died happy in the Lord—Peace be to her ashes—So mote it be.

Samuel Bean's second wife was Susanna Clegg, born between Wellesley and Crosshill in 1840. She and Samuel had a daughter, also named Susanna, before she died, on April 27, 1867 at the age of twenty-seven. The two wives are buried side by side. Their husband prepared a cryptogram, similar although not identical to that on Henrietta's funeral card. It was fifteen letters across and fifteen down, carved on a white marble stone (Lamb and Brown). The reader must solve the puzzle by reading in a zigzag fashion. It reads (with spelling discrepancies).

In memoriam of Henrietta, 1st wife of S. Bean, M.D. who died 27 September 1865, age 23 years, 2 months and 17 days and Susanna his 2nd wife who died 27 April, 1867, aged 26 years, 10 months, and 15 days, 2 better wives 1 man never had, they were gifts from God but are now in Heaven. May God help me so to meet them there.

Reader Meet us in Heaven.

The inscription was first decoded by cemetery caretaker John Hammond in 1947. The Victorian stone has weathered badly. Wellesley Township and the Wellesley Historical Society were responsible for the duplication of the unusual marker, this time in durable gray granite. The letters are picked out in black so that anyone wishing to study and solve the puzzle may do so with ease. The duplicate was erected in 1982, so that people could better read the inscription and solve the puzzle.

LOUISE THE UNFORTUNATE

In cemeteries and graveyards across America loving tributes are erected so that family and friends will be remembered and not forgotten. Ornately carved tombstones, carefully inscribed and delicately placed, mark the final resting places of their loved ones.

Ghost hunters and visitors often stumble upon tombstones that sometimes defy explanation. Although someone placed a tombstone at the deceased's gravesite it may lack the traditional information that surrounding markers display.

It is entirely possible that their life story as well as their real names or full names were never known. Maybe they were strangers in a new land, or preferred to remain incognito. This often resulted in folklore and legends being connected to their mysterious gravesites. Truth is often stranger than fiction, and rumors and folk memory are passed from one generation to the next, confusing the issue even more.

One such mysterious tombstone is located in the Natchez, Mississippi City Cemetery (Whitington, 2005). To add to the mystique of the deceased, "Louise the Unfortunate" is all that is inscribed on her tombstone. Adding even more to the mystery of who she was, a rare mysterious rose bush blooms year round at the head of her tombstone, as if to say, "Notice me—I am somebody!" Folklore and legend tell the story of a young woman named Louise who came to Natchez to be married. Although it has never been proven where she came from, it is known that she arrived in Natchez by steamboat. The steamboat docked at Natchez "Under-the-Hill," the most notorious part of town. It is located below the bluff of the great Mississippi River. It was well documented as a hell-raising mecca for men who wanted liquor, women, gambling, and a good fight to even out their good times. It became a gathering place for riverboat captains and their crews, boatmen, planters, trappers, fat merchants, harlots, and river rats. Just as numerous in the taverns and dance halls were card sharks, thieves, murderers, and other fugitives from justice. It was also the red-light district of Natchez and these men frequented the bordellos and bawdy houses day and night.

Above the Hill, there existed a tranquil city. Tree-lined streets with elegant Victorian homes set it worlds apart from the squalor below. This was the town that Louise was to call home. However, the gentleman she was to marry never showed up to meet her. Distraught and upset, she began a citywide search for her fiancé. He was nowhere to be found.

Because she never found him and perhaps because she was clinging to the hope that he would one day come to find her in Natchez, she chose to stay. Maybe she was too embarrassed to return home with her reputation in question. Whatever the reason she was left with few choices and little resources for survival in a town that was beautiful and exciting, yet dark and dangerous.

In the beginning, although she was devastated, alone, and bereft, she was able to find respectable work as a housekeeper and seamstress. However, she was eventually lured under the hill to work as a barmaid in local taverns. With the passage of time she slipped even lower into darkness and despair and with the memories of her fiancé pushed even deeper into the dark recesses of her soul, she became a "Scarlet Woman."

Even though life under the hill was hard, rumor has it that she was befriended by a local doctor who treated her kindly during her years as a prostitute. He is also supposedly the one who paid her funeral expenses. Of course, time and historical inaccuracies only add more questions to the mystery. Other legends say that a wealthy plantation owner paid for her funeral expenses and had her tombstone placed in the cemetery.

However questionable the events that unfolded, one fact remains: she obviously meant something to someone because she was not buried in a potter's field. Although it is assumed that she was destitute and alone, perhaps she was not as unfortunate as many believed. Perhaps she was loved by someone secretly.

Her now-famous gravesite is accented with a beautiful antique rose bush that some people believe was brought over from Bermuda. Who was the person who planted this very prolific rose at Louise's gravesite? Perhaps one key to the mystery can be found in a tradition long associated with Wales. It is a Welsh custom to plant flowers and roses on the graves of their loved ones. Was the person who planted this rare spice rose Welsh?

The spice rose, as it is now known, is a lovely light pink-almond color imbued with a heady spicy fragrance. Could it be that this spicy scent appealed to a man's sense of remembrance? Could it be that her fiancé finally found his way to her, only to learn of her tragic circumstances? Could he have planted the rose as an expression of his love for her?

Sadly, she may still search for her fiancé, since many people have reported seeing the ghost of a young woman dressed in period clothing wandering around in the cemetery late at night. She always appears near the section of the cemetery where Louise is buried, looking confused and sorrowful.

MURDERED BY HUMAN WOLVES

Pottawatomie County, Oklahoma is the final resting place of a mysterious young woman named Katherine Cross. Just as puzzling and unusual is her tombstone with its cryptic epitaph.

Katherine Cross
dau of J. T. & M. K. Cross
Mar. 13, 1899
Oct. 10, 1917
Murdered by Human Wolves

Over time people probably forgot her name and perhaps even where she lived. However, rumors, speculation, and folklore may never cease to exist regarding how she died. Perhaps these rumors play a part in keeping her alive in ghostly form. Now, almost a hundred years later, people still seek answers to the cause of her tragic death.

As memories faded with time, her death and the circumstances surrounding it have become a local mystery, which remain unsolved to this day. Theories about her cryptic epitaph are as widespread and varied as the people who stumble upon it. Whether it is read in the daylight, or as the approaching darkness surrounds it, there is no discounting the fact that it will evoke anxiety and possibly fear as one conjures up images of werewolves hiding in the woods nearby. There have been many reports of wolves howling as people approach her gravesite.

Evidently, at one time there were many such epitaphs on grave markers in and around Seminole County, Oklahoma dating from the same time period. However, they have been defaced, stolen, or are simply no longer readable.

After learning of this tombstone in Konawa, Oklahoma, I could hardly wait for an opportunity to see it for myself. "Murdered by Human Wolves," became my next cemetery mystery (www.waymarking.com, www.findagrave.com). So we set out on yet another investigation, and as usual Sharon, Tammy, Lisa, and I were not disappointed.

We arrived at the cemetery very late in the afternoon, even though we had given ourselves plenty of time to get there. One cemetery after another in the towns we passed through delayed us quite a bit, almost too much. When we finally arrived at our destination we encountered not one, but two cemeteries across the road from each other. Not knowing which one held Katherine's grave, we wasted a lot of time at the wrong cemetery. Tired and hot, but by no means discouraged, we entered the second cemetery.

I noticed as we drove into the cemetery that a white truck had pulled up along the side of the cemetery and stopped. I felt a little apprehensive for some reason but just passed it off to being tired and anxious to find Katherine's tombstone before dark. We all fanned out in different directions, looking for her gravesite, but I couldn't keep from looking over my shoulder at the truck. It was very hot and the driver peered at us from inside the truck. It wasn't long before Sharon picked up on his presence and she too became concerned about his watchful gaze. We didn't want to alarm the other girls so we silently watched him watching us while we continued our search.

Finally Lisa called to us that she had found it. We all rushed to where she was standing. I for one was amazed to actually see the tombstone exactly as it was described. It was one thing to hear about it, but to really see the inscription "Murdered by Human Wolves" was quite another. Suddenly, I was covered in goose bumps and I knew instinctively that someone else was nearby, watching us, and I wasn't wrong! I turned to see that a second truck had pulled up alongside the white one. Now there were two trucks and two men watching us from their enclosed vehicles.

Sharon and I both sensed them at the same time and arrived at the same conclusion. Things were not normal. The fact that they were watching us was no coincidence. We both agreed that we needed to leave before dark to insure our safety. Although I was reluctant to leave Katherine's tombstone, I had achieved my goal. I got the photographic evidence I had come for. I would have liked to record an EVP and possibly taken more pictures after dark, but intuition and prior experiences made me increasingly wary that we were about to experience something paranormal and perhaps sinister, or worse.

So we got back into the car and headed out of the cemetery in the opposite direction of the trucks. Thankfully there was another exit. One last look in the direction of the men watching us made me shudder. They were still sitting there observing us, and I think it was their piercing gazes that heightened my intuition of their perhaps less-than-benevolent presence. Were they werewolves?

Neither Sharon nor I are given to hysterics. We have experienced too much and seen even more. Because of that, I feel we can trust our intuitions and recognize impending danger when we encounter it. The men were there for a reason. But what reason? Their presence was certainly no coincidence and I sincerely feel that if we had remained until nightfall, we might not have been able to leave.

Local legend has it that Katherine Cross was found deep in the woods, her body badly mangled and shredded. Many people believe even today that she fell victim to a pack of werewolves, or at the very least one very powerful, ferocious werewolf. There is also widespread gossip and speculation that she was murdered by members of the Ku Klux Klan. However, my research reveals that the Klan did not make a concerted national effort to recruit in Oklahoma until 1920 after establishing a strong Texas membership base. So we can probably rule them out.

In the October 25, 1917 edition of the *Seminole County News*, an article stated that Katherine Cross died as the result of a botched operation. The short article revealed that Dr. A. H. Yates of Konawa was arrested for performing a criminal operation on Katherine; presumably an abortion. Evidently the operation led to her death. The article ended by saying that Dr. Yates had been charged two months earlier with the same offense (www.findagrave.com).

Evidently Dr. Yates and Fred O'Neal, a school teacher from Konawa, were held in the county jail for the death of eighteen-year-old Elise Stone. She had been admitted to Dr. Yates' office on August 15, where she remained for four days, at which time she was taken to his home. Her death, according to Dr. Yates, was the result of a congestive chill. Although most of Konawa was satisfied with Dr. Yates' pronouncement, the few who were suspicious contacted county attorney A. G. Nichols. Nichols and the county physician, along with an order by M. L. Rascoe, Justice of the Peace, dug up Elise to perform an autopsy on her. This autopsy was actually preformed in the graveyard. It was declared that she had died due to complications from yet another criminal operation. Just two months later, Katherine Cross would suffer the same fate. Why would he perform another abortion if he had just been jailed for performing one which resulted in the death of Elise?

As I stood there looking at her enigmatic tombstone I had to wonder if she and Elise were not victims in more ways than one. Could it be that Dr. Yates and Fred O'Neal were werewolf hunters? Could it be that the doctor was aborting werewolf fetuses? Could his determination to prevent any more births of werewolves have overridden any fear of incarceration? I think this is a very real possibility. And if my suppositions are correct, one has to wonder how many other young men and women had fallen prey to their sinister plot to destroy werewolves living in and around Seminole County, Oklahoma in the early 1900s.

There are many unanswered questions and just as many unsubstantiated rumors surrounding the mysterious deaths of Katherine Cross and Elise Stone. If you are as intrigued and as curious as I am perhaps you will want to explore this cemetery mystery before Katherine's tombstone disappears into the mysterious world of paranormal oblivion.

TOMBSTONE IMAGE

Not all images or symbols that appear on tombstones are engraved or sculpted by stonemasons. Some may suddenly appear as paranormal representations of communication. Visitors and ghost hunters alike have often seen faces, full-bodied images, names (other than those engraved on the marker), and any number of objects such as images associated with sudden, mysterious, and otherwise unnatural deaths. This can be very disconcerting, especially if they appear spontaneously on a moonlit night. Many such images have been photographed and add mystery and intrigue to an otherwise traditional tombstone. Of course seeing is believing—until I saw and photographed one such image myself, it was hard even for me to understand this phenomenon. The following story is one such example.

Our team was exploring a city cemetery late one night for possible paranormal activity. Several people had reported seeing a huge red orb in the cemetery, and as always my curiosity was engaged. While wandering around and actually a little bored I checked out tombstone after tombstone. The cemetery appeared quiet and peaceful, and the elusive red orb that had been witnessed by visitors and mourners was just that, illusive.

I was almost to the back of the cemetery when a tombstone caught my attention. It had one of our family surnames name on it, and always a genealogist at heart, I stopped to see if there might be a connection. Much to my amazement as I was standing there reading the accompanying inscription the image of a young man appeared right in the center of the tombstone. I was shocked, to say the least. First of all it was totally unexpected, and second, my left brain went immediately into its logical debunker mode: reflection on the marble, lights from somewhere creating the effect, just my imagination, and so on.

Why is it sometimes so hard to accept the obvious? The image didn't disappear. It stayed there and became sharper as time elapsed. It was of a young man wearing a baseball cap who appeared to be about the same age as the deceased. I was able to photograph this amazing phenomenon, and he appeared for all the world as if he could just walk right out of the tombstone.

I was really excited and called for other members of our group to come and see. Only two could see him on the tombstone, however they could all see him on my digital camera. "How'd you do that?" they asked in unison. The obvious answer was of course, I didn't do it. He did! He was obviously attempting to communicate with me, and perhaps he had a message to share, but I was so stunned I probably altered my vibrational reception and could not hear or receive it.

I have been back several times to see if I could recapture his image, but unfortunately so many phenomenal events can't be replicated. To do so would require that I was operating in the exact same vibrational frequency and evidently I was not. The atmospheric conditions would have to be exactly the same and the ghost of this young man would need to have the same desire to communicate as he did on that particular night. That's a lot of energy to manifest.

Still, it happened. It was witnessed by others and I was gifted with a new form of paranormal communication. For this I am very grateful.

The more I explore the fields of ghost hunting and paranormal research, the more I am aware of the fact that there is no death and we do not die! We are merely transformed into a finer vibrational frequency, where we can still see, hear, and make contact with others.

TEN
CEMETERY
MONUMENTS

When I first began ghost hunting I was somewhat confused by the terms tombstones, headstones, tombs, crypts, monuments, vaults, and mausoleums because I have heard these terms used individually and even interchangeably in many cases.

I have had my own personal experiences and heard others' accounts of ghosts appearing and disappearing in cemeteries and more specifically at one particular gravesite. Of course, these mysterious gravesites are usually defined by a marker which may figure in the haunting in some way.

I have decided to include in this chapter some definitions that will help you relate to cemetery markers and how they play a part in haunts and ghostly sightings.

1. *Headstone:* A headstone is a slab of stone, marble, or granite placed at the grave where the head of the deceased rests. At many gravesites a footstone is also used to mark the end of the grave. Traditionally the headstone is engraved with the name and dates of birth and death. Footstones are usually inscribed with the deceased's initials or position in the family, such as Mother or Father. Footstones may also be placed at the end of the grave and engraved with information indicating military service. Today most cemeteries prefer only headstones because they allow for easier maintenance.

2. *Tombstone:* In earlier times markers were usually referred to as gravestones. They are usually upright slabs of marble, granite, or stone, with rounded, pointed, arched, or gabled artistically shaped tops. From Puritan times tombstones have been carved with symbolic reminders

of death such as winged skulls, cherubic angels, gruesome faces, and any number of images that indicated the passage from life to death. Today it is easy to find tombstones engraved with more elaborate allegorical imagery such as images of fleeting time or designs representing the deceased's trade, hobby, or professional status.

As nineteenth century tombstone art became more diverse, tombstones ranged from plain, unadorned, and contemporary to those that were ornately decorated. Crosses and angels began to show up on tombstones and actually became tombstones themselves as they became taller, wider, and more artistically designed. Celtic crosses and unique and impressive statuary are a good example of the changing trends in tombstone art. How gravesites are marked today has evolved from the simple boulders and wooden crosses of the past.

3. *Crypt:* A crypt is a stone chamber, tunnel, or huge underground enclosure usually situated beneath the floor of a church, castle, or monastery. They were used in medieval times for burials and contained sarcophagus, coffins, and mummified bodies. Some churches were built above ground level so that crypts could be placed beneath them at ground level. Although crypts are usually found under churches and cathedrals they can also be found under mausoleums and chapels on huge private estates. Wealthy families often have family crypts in which all members of the family are entombed.

4. *Monument:* A monument can be defined as a statue, a building, or other artistic structure erected to com-

memorate a person, a group of people, or an event. These magnificent structures are used in cemeteries to memorialize people who have died. They are more often than not designed to convey information about a person or event. They could have been nobility, prestigious or famous people, or heroes. Monuments are also used to define certain areas within a cemetery such as religious areas and fraternal orders, as well as cultural divisions. They are also erected in remembrance of groups of people who lost their lives together as in fires, explosions, or natural disasters, in which case a mass burial may have necessitated a single burial site.

5. *Mausoleum:* A mausoleum is a free-standing building constructed as a memorial. It encompasses the interment space or burial chamber for a deceased person or persons. Traditionally these buildings are large and impressive, and are usually constructed by people of wealth and status. However smaller versions can be just as elaborate and extraordinary. These smaller architecturally designed structures were popular with those who were less affluent. Mausoleums are magnificent buildings with a roof and sometimes a door for additional interments or visitors' access. A single mausoleum may be permanently sealed. In addition to containing the body or bodies of the deceased they may also provide space for cremated remains with additional crematory niches inside.

6. *Tomb:* A tomb is a repository for the remains of the dead. The term generally refers to any structurally enclosed

interment space or burial chamber of varying sizes. Tomb is actually a word used in a broader sense to encompass a number of interment places.

Chest Tombs: These unusual tombs commonly stand over the grave or burial site rather than containing the actual body. Chest or box tombs look like a small one-person, above ground, elongated box. The body is usually beneath a base of brick or stone on top of which is an inscribed slab. Regardless of how it looks, the box or chest type tomb is actually empty, and the body is buried underneath it.

Table Top Tomb: This is another type of tomb which looks like a stone table. This is also a false tomb and the body rests beneath it. The table top is a flat inscribed slab that rests on four or six pillars and dates back to colonial times. The only real purpose behind this type of tomb was to protect the grave from vandals, grave robbers, animals, and natural disasters.

7. *Vault:* A vault is a lined enclosure that is used to hold the casket. In earlier times vaults were used to hold the deceased until graves could be dug or as a keeping place until family members arrived from afar. Today burial vaults are used to hold the casket at the time of interment. The vault is lowered into the grave first, and the casket is then placed within the vault.

THE MERCHANT ORB

The Marion Cemetery located in Marion, Ohio is the home of the much talked about, analyzed, and studied "Merchant Ball" (www.flickr.com, and www.graveaddictions.com).

When the town of Marion, Ohio was founded, land for a cemetery was dedicated to the public by the affluent proprietors of the newly founded township. After about twenty-five years it was found that the old burial grounds were too small and inconveniently located. It was also deemed unsuitable due to its flat surface and the undesirable fact that the land held water, leaving the grounds soggy and wet.

The town had not only encroached upon the graveyard but actually grown beyond it. The railroad had also intruded upon the peace and tranquility of the serene cemetery. As a result of these inconveniences a town meeting was called in 1857 and it was decided that another cemetery site should be chosen. The new, more attractive, and much better-suited site consisted of about fifty acres with more adjacent land to be annexed as needed.

Marion Cemetery is very large and the Merchant monument is located in the oldest section of its extensive grounds. The older part is situated on the north side of Vernon Heights Boulevard. It is very well maintained and as with many older graveyards it has a history of being haunted.

The Merchant monument boasts an intriguing history of strange reverberating sounds, weird sightings, unusual happenings at the gravesite, and the mysterious spinning of the sphere that sits on top of the monument.

This unique tombstone monument has received a great deal of attention for well over one hundred years. In 1929 the Merchant Ball achieved international fame with its coverage by Ripley's *Believe it or Not*. Of course it's no wonder that Ripley would find this fascinating, especially since his very first job was as a tombstone engraver.

This magnificent orb was erected by Charles Merchant as a monument for his family plot. Surely his wealth and status added to this infamous spinning sphere. It was created with a five-foot pedestal base measuring about thirty inches square at the top. A huge granite orb that weighs 5,200 pounds and is three feet in diameter sits on the top of the pedestal. However, it does not just sit there! It rotates inexplicably about two to five inches every year. It moves from one century into the next with mysterious unexplained consistency.

Many people believe a restless spirit keeps the ball in motion, while others have tried in vain to determine a more scientific explanation. However, the fact remains to this day that no one really knows why it moves.

During the demolition of an old home place, a fascinating photograph of the Merchant Ball was found beneath a staircase. In the photograph it appears that the gigantic orb is being magically lifted or levitated by some unknown energy force or vibrational frequency. Was this incredible photograph hidden, or could it have been just stored away for safe keeping only to be forgotten as the years passed? (This incredible photo can been seen at www.GhosttoGhost.com.)

One has to wonder if the placement of the giant sphere and its surrounding eleven smaller orbs (which serve as grave markers) are not pointing to a greater secret. One is instantly reminded of a solar system when viewing the monument, and of course how could the ancient stone circles not be envisioned? Does the placement of orbs set up a vibrational vortex or portal opening into another realm? Why are there only eleven smaller orbs? Were there ever twelve? Why are they set in a semi-circle? Was there at one time a complete circle around the sphere? Does the monument set on a ley line? Does the fact that C. B. Merchant was a Mason have anything to do with the unique design of his family plot?

The questions are as endless and as enigmatic as the man who erected the memorial to his family. Research has revealed very little about him. Perhaps he intended to evoke a mystifying atmosphere so others would contemplate the sphere for years to come. There is no doubt that the monument is as distinguished as he was.

Since its erection in 1896, it has continued to move in a slow deliberate rotation. Its movement was first noticed by Mr. Merchant himself along with the cemetery sexton in 1898, just two years after its placement. They discovered that it had moved slightly, exposing the unpolished spot where it sat on the pedestal. This was obvious because the huge sphere was evidently polished after it was set, leaving a smooth unpolished spot that was exposed as the ball revolved. The ball has never been securely fastened as far as anyone knows. It was decided after the rotation was observed that the ball should be reset. This was done in 1898 in an effort to stop the ball from spinning. However, as fate would have it, the ball began its slow movement once again, defying any attempts to stop its journey into the unknown.

The ball was again examined in 1905. At that time the highest point reached by the unpolished spot was twenty-two inches from the base's sitting position. Some time after these measurements were taken it had once again moved eastward and downward fifteen to twenty inches toward the corner of the base.

Theories, stories, folklore, and bizarre explanations abound as to why it continues to move so slowly, demanding attention and recognition. There have been countless non-paranormal explanations as well as paranormal ones for the ball's odd movement, ranging anywhere from vibrational frequencies to other-worldly forces. None of these, of course, satisfactorily explain the movement of the ball, although it has been tested by scientists from around the world without conclusive results. Several theories have been put forth over the years in an attempt to explain this incredible phenomenon.

The firm that erected the giant sphere attributed the movement of the ball to mineral deposits (quartz, feldspar, and mica) within the granite ball. They reported that these minerals brought the center of gravity away from the center of the ball. It is highly possible that the amount of quartz and the quality of quartz could affect the rotation of the ball.

Some people have attributed the ball's movement to the Coriolis Effect, which is by definition the deflection effect of the earth's rotation on any object in motion which diverts it to the right of velocity in the Northern Hemisphere and to the left in the Southern Hemisphere. However, it is doubtful that it had anything to do with the Coriolis Effect as the unpolished spot moves erratically and not in a straight line at a right angle to the earth's movement.

In a letter to a member of the Marion Cemetery Association, state geologist Edward Orton Jr. said that movement of the ball is probably due to one of two reasons. First the ball may become more heated than the heavy base and therefore expand more, causing it to rotate slightly. The contraction might not be sufficient enough to take up the displacement caused by the heat received earlier in the day. Secondly, one may regard the circumference of the sphere as lengthening out on one side and giving rise to a pulling stress between the ball and the base upon which it rests. It has been suggested that the monument is partly shaded during a portion of the day and that there is some connection between this fact and the rotation of the ball.

Yet another theory suggests that as the base becomes more heated it expands, somewhat nudging the ball on the south side, and amid the contraction and cooling again draws the ball southward.

Granted it could be the result of the ever-changing temperatures causing the base of the monument to expand and contract. However, there are absolutely no scratches which one would expect to see from the rotation of the ball against its pedestal. It would appear that the moving of the granite ball against the stone of the pedestal would most assuredly mar the surface of the sphere, yet not a blemish can be seen after a century of its rotating. The ball is still as pristinely polished as it was over one hundred years ago.

Due to all the controversy surrounding the ball, one would expect to hear something about a hoax or vandalism. No evidence of a hoax has ever been uncovered or identified—not surprising since heavy machinery and equipment would be required to raise or move the ball.

The ball's gigantic size has impelled more than one visitor to ask what would happen if the ball suddenly rolls off its pedestal? Its immense size would surely crush someone easily, dissuading any pranksters.

The Merchant Ball is truly a cemetery mystery. Will it continue its perpetual spinning throughout the ages? What's your theory?

THE KILLOUGH MONUMENT

I had heard about the Killough Monument for years and always wondered if the ghostly phenomena surrounding it were true or merely local legend (Whitington, 2005, and www.flickr.com). I had been told about an apparition of an Indian Chief who startles unsuspecting visitors, appearing in a magnificent headdress and full battle regalia. He is always seen riding a large white horse, and as soon as eye contact is made he disappears.

In addition to the ghostly apparition of the Indian Chief, visitors to the monument have also experienced varied supernatural phenomena. The site seems colder even on the hottest days of summer. The terrified screams of men, women, and children can be heard, and seem to originate from all sides of the monument. The eerie feeling that everyone seems to experience at the site sets the tone for the atmosphere surrounding the monument.

My research revealed that in 1837 a man named Isaac Killough moved about thirty members of his extended family by wagon train from Talladega, Alabama to East Texas, after purchasing land grants from the newly formed Republic of Texas.

On December 24, 1837 Isaac Killough arrived in Texas with his four sons; Isaac Jr., Allen, Samuel, Nathaniel, and their families. Also in the party were George Wood who was married to Jane Killough, and their five children, as well as Polly Killough, her husband Owen Williams, and his two brothers Elbert and Barakias (Kias) Williams. Kias was soon to wed Isaac Killough's youngest daughter Elisabeth.

Over the next several months the Killough, Wood, and Williams families cleared the land, built houses and barns, planted crops, and worked their fields. Although the Cherokee Indians had befriended the Killough clan, their allies, the Kickapoo, who lived in a village just a mere six miles from them, resented the fact that the Killough party had settled on land that had previously belonged to the tribe.

By August 1838 it became increasingly apparent that the local Indians, as well as a band of Indians and Mexicans, were becoming a growing threat to the settlers. Just after noon on October 5, 1838 a band of renegade Indians attacked eighteen members of the Killough clan as they were returning to work in their fields. Isaac Killough was killed in his front yard as his family and friends were massacred all around him.

In November 1838, Nathaniel Killough, who had escaped the raiding party with his wife and one-year-old daughter led a group to return home and bury the bodies of his family. Only his brother Samuel could be identified by a gold tooth. The bodies of the Killough, Wood, and Williams families were buried under a large oak tree a few hundred yards east of the senior Killough's homestead. In 1930 the WPA erected a twenty-five-foot stone monument in the shape of a pyramid at the site where Nathaniel had buried his family members. In 1965 the cemetery where the monument is located was dedicated as a Texas Historical Landmark. The Killough massacre was the largest Indian depredation in East Texas and resulted in the Cherokee and their allies being forced out of Texas.

I was curious as to why an Indian chief would haunt this particular monument. Evidently no Indians were killed in the raid because none of the Killough clan were armed. So why would a ghost of an Indian chief appear at this particular monument? It is entirely possible that he could have been killed in battle on land that previously belonged to the Indians. However, I would like to propose another theory.

Rumor and local legend, as well as historical research, seems to support the fact that after George Wood was murdered, his wife and five children were taken into captivity by the raiding party that fateful day. Also historically documented and recorded is the fact that one of the Woods boys was taken in by a Plains Indian tribe and later became a chief. What is even more interesting and adds validity to the story is the fact that the original land purchased by Isaac Killough was considered too dangerous for settlement at the time because of marauding Plains Indians. Because of this they chose instead to exchange their land grants for land near the Neches River.

Given this information it is entirely possible that one of the Wood boys did indeed become a chief and if this is true, it is also plausible that his ghost would return to the place where his father and other family members were massacred. Perhaps he needs this energy connection.

Any place where a horrific tragedy took place, such as a massacre, would retain strong energy imprints, as well as residual energy. These energies can be felt, seen, and heard by visitors who are sensitive to energy in all its varied forms of manifestation.

Personal Note:

Many years ago a guide on a large white horse appeared to me. He was dressed in full chiefly attire, including a magnificent headdress. His thunderous voice shocked me to the very core of my being as he literally shouted, "I am Walks in Woods, I am strong! I am a Mandan Indian." For days after he appeared to me I would jump at every noise I heard, and it took me years to assimilate his energy to the point where communication could be established.

Over the years he has given me advice and shared many stories of his life and the spiritual nature of the Mandan Indians. He has also given me information on a very unique form of divination which I plan to publish in the near future.

By now you are probably wondering how this experience is related to the Killough Monument and the Indian Chief who appears there.

My great-great-grandfather was from Alabama and married a young girl from the Killough clan, also from Alabama. They migrated to East Texas during the same time frame. I haven't connected all the dots, yet, but I intuitively know that the families are connected.

My very powerful guide, Walks in Woods, is a Mandan Indian, which is a Plains Indian tribe. Just a coincidence you might say. However, I know that there are no coincidences and every thing we encounter has reason and purpose in our lives. Are Walk in Woods and the spirited Indian Chief one and the same? Are they connected to me through spiritual family ties? It remains to be seen.

MERIWETHER LEWIS MONUMENT

In September 1806, the Lewis and Clark expedition returned to St. Louis after an absence of over two years. Lewis had explored over six thousand miles of wilderness and had written journal after journal about what he encountered on his journey. After Lewis returned to Washington he was appointed governor of the Louisiana Territory (Taylor, 2003).

However, he soon became disillusioned with this appointment. He found corruption and abuses within this political arena. The government denied his vouchers for medicine for the Indians and as a result he went into debt to pay for the medicine out of his own pocket.

He became angry and frustrated with a government that would not support his idealism, and wrote angry letters to Washington. Feeling a need to defend his motives he decided to go to Washington. His original plan was to go down the Mississippi by boat from New Orleans to Washington. However, he altered his plans and opted instead to travel along the

Natchez Trace, a rough and often dangerous wilderness route. His traveling companion was Cherokee Indian agent Major John Neely. They set off with two of his servants and two pack mules to carry his records and journals.

On October 10, 1809 a heavy rainstorm fell on the party. The violent thunderstorm sent the pack mules fleeing into the forest. Major Neely beseeched Lewis to ride to the nearest cabin on the trail. Lewis agreed to stay over night at the home of John Grinder, which sometimes served as a wayside inn for travelers. Major Neely promised to help find the runaway mules and disappeared into the forest.

When Lewis arrived at the Grinder home, Mr. Grinder was away on business, but Mrs. Grinder let him in. A short time later the servants arrived with the pack mules, and they were told they could sleep in the barn. She prepared a bed for Lewis—however, he preferred to sleep on the floor on his buffalo robe.

According to Mrs. Grinder's account, she heard Lewis pacing across the floor, walking back and forth and talking to himself. In the middle of the night she heard a gunshot, and then the sound of something heavy hitting the floor. And then she heard the words, "Oh Lord!"

Almost immediately afterwards she heard a second gunshot. Then she heard Lewis at her door. He was begging her, "Oh Madame, give me some water and heal my wounds." Mrs. Grinder refused to leave the room to offer him any assistance. She actually waited more than two hours before sending one of her children out to the barn to wake his servants. They came inside and found Lewis back on his blood-soaked buffalo robe pallet. He whispered to them, "I am no coward, but I am strong. So hard to die!" He died shortly thereafter and those were the last words he ever spoke.

Major Neely arrived later that morning. He immediately sent a messenger with a note to the president. "It is with extreme pain that I have to inform you of the death of his Excellency Meriwether Lewis, Governor of Louisiana who died on the morning of the 11th instant and I am sorry to say by suicide. I had him as decently buried as I could in that same place. If there is anything wished by his friends to be done to his grave I will attend to their instructions." Lewis was buried on the Grinder's property. Neely took charge of Lewis' journals and personally carried them the rest of the way to Washington. His journals were turned over to Thomas Jefferson.

Most historians would say that he committed suicide, but did he? A major conspiracy and cover up is more probable.

1. The first and only account of the shooting comes from Mrs. Grinder, a person who would not even help him in his direst moment, as he lay dying in her house, choosing instead to wait two hours before sending for help. And one has to wonder what kind of business Mr. Grinder was away on.

2. It was Major Neely who conveniently disappeared all night in the middle of a violent thunderstorm. Where did he stay? He is the one who decided that Lewis committed suicide. He was the one who immediately sent word to Jefferson. He is the one who had him buried immediately, without respect to his position or national recognition. He is the one who delivered Lewis'

journals and records to Washington. One has to wonder exactly what was recorded in those journal or records. Were they worth murdering Lewis for? Neely is the one who arrived shortly after Lewis died to clean up/cover up the tragedy.

3. Why didn't the servants hear the two gunshots? Or did they, but were kept restrained and possibly threatened to keep them in the barn until they were called for?

4. If Lewis did indeed shoot himself, not once but twice, why would he beg Mrs. Grinder to help him? We're talking about a military man, a great adventurer, a wilderness pioneer who lived with the Indians, hunted buffalo, battled the great Missouri River and helped shape America. Don't you believe this man would know how to shoot himself where he would die swiftly, instead of once in the side and then in the head where he would suffer in agony?

There can be little doubt that Meriwether Lewis was murdered, and this is probably why the ghost of Lewis still wanders the area where he died. People have seen strange light configurations near his monument. They have heard on occasion a man's voice whispering, "So hard to die!"

The mystery of his death is still unsolved and he still wanders the grounds where he was murdered. Perhaps he is seeking comfort and someone to ease the pain and suffering of betrayal from those he trusted most.

ELEVEN
CEMETERY
MAUSOLEUMS

The word *mausoleum* comes to us from a man named Mausolus, who was the king of Halicarnassus, a great harbor city in Asia (www.unmuseum.org/maus).

When Mausolus died in 353 BCE his wife was devastated and as a tribute to him she had a spectacular mausoleum built in his memory. She spared no expense building this impressive 140-foot structure on a hill overlooking the city he had envisioned and created, adding even more prestigious height to its already astounding stature. From below it was a sight to behold as it sat majestically inside a beautifully manicured courtyard.

Unfortunately this regal mausoleum that became the eponym for mausoleums worldwide was destroyed by a series of earthquakes in 1400 AD. This resulted in the total destruction of the mausoleum, leaving only the platform of the once famous building that was heralded as one of the "Seven Wonders of the World."

Historically, mausoleums were large impressive structures for deceased leaders and famous people. They also left a legacy for the rich and famous who adopted the mausoleum as an ostentatious show of wealth and power in cemeteries across Europe and America. Mausoleums became popular with landed gentry and nobility in the United States and many countries in Europe. Although traditionally large and heavily ornamented, there were also smaller versions with doors that could be sealed. These simple intimate versions were erected for people with less status and money. Mausoleums usually enclose a burial chamber that is either entirely above ground or within a burial vault below the structure. Older mausoleums usually contained the body or several bodies, probably within sarcophagi or interment niches. Today mausoleums may also act as columbaria (a type of mausoleum for cremated remains) with additional built-in cinerary urn niches.

While tombstones and headstones are the traditional types of grave markers in cemeteries and graveyards they are not the only way to mark a grave. Many huge, ornate mausoleums that are often overwhelming in size and architectural design mark gravesites of the deceased. To me, one of the scariest things about cemeteries are these enormous, elaborate structures. The very thought of a body or bodies being entombed inside dark gothic structures is spine-tingling. Many people cringe at the thought of being locked away forever, even in death. I have never met anyone who really likes the idea of being interred in these dark creepy tombs. Today, people would much rather be cremated than confined in mausoleums.

These expensive tombs enjoyed great popularity during the Victorian era. They became the exclusive resting places of prominent townsfolk and the wealthy elite. On occasion the deceased was cremated and the urn that held the ashes was placed inside the mausoleum. However, traditionally the casket was placed on a stone platform inside. Most mausoleums are kept locked and usually the cemetery caretaker or a specific family member holds the key.

It's really spooky at night to chance upon a huge gothic mausoleum in a darkened cemetery. One is almost instantly drawn to its massive ornate doors and it's not hard to envision them swinging open as a ghost, vampire, or something worse steps out. This is even scarier when they have glass doors allowing mourners and visitors to see inside—many of these still exist in cemeteries across America.

It's not uncommon to see flower arrangements, furniture, photographs, and personal items that belonged to the deceased inside the chamber. In a sense it is almost like glancing into someone's house. Although sparsely furnished, the one defining object is always the casket that holds the remains of the body whose spirit still may linger there.

To many people, mausoleums represent the ultimate devastation, the end of life as we know it. In death, the deceased enters a door that has been opened and then sealed shut forever. This finality is too frightening for many to accept.

These massive cemetery structures were erected for a number of reasons. Although their original design was to meet the obligation of a decent burial and define the final resting places of the deceased, their presence in the cemetery is an overwhelming display of wealth and power.

History is replete with stories of ghosts in cemeteries, especially associated with tombs. One only has to spend some time in New Orleans to grasp the mystery and madness surrounding archaic mausoleums.

MARIE LAVEAUX'S MYSTERIOUS WISHING TOMB

Deep in southern Louisiana are the "Cemeteries of the Dead," as people often refer to cemeteries in New Orleans. These cemeteries are crowded with one mausoleum after another—rows and rows of unique above-ground mansions for the deceased.

The first time I visited the St. Louis Cemetery Number 1, I was thirteen years old and living with my father and younger brother in New Orleans. My father, who had a deep appreciation and respect for the deceased, took me to the historic cemetery to see the unusual tombs and eccentric shrines of the dead. Even today it's hard for me to see an old cemetery without wanting to stop and walk among the aging tombstones and mausoleums. I was fascinated, terrified, and forever impressed by the unique, eerie mausoleums I saw there. I will never forget how they looked, smelled, and spoke to me as I passed by one after another. If you are seeking mystery, intrigue, and cemetery ghosts then you must visit the cemeteries in New Orleans.

In the Crescent City most of the cemeteries consist of elevated vaults and tombs. Although they are more expensive than traditional tombstones and underground burials, they are necessary because of the location of the city. The water table beneath the city of New Orleans became a major issue during its formative years. At one time or another throughout history its cemeteries were completely inundated. Saint Peter's cemetery, established in 1721 and located in the French Quarter, began with in-ground graves. The newly founded Creole society soon realized the futility of this practice as many graves lower than the adjacent swamps rapidly filled with water. Soon heavy rains and flooding caused caskets to surface. This posed serious health problems for the newly formed city and immediately prompted citizens to create new ways of burying their dead. Above-ground interments were the answer and grew into an accepted practice, creating cemeteries full of unique, and less traditional burial spaces and unusual mausoleums to fascinate and intrigue mourners and visitors alike.

History is replete with stories of ghosts in cemeteries, especially associated with mausoleums. A person only needs to spend a few days in New Orleans to grasp the mysteries and secrets surrounding these magnificent antiquated mausoleums.

One of the most famous mausoleums in New Orleans is located in St. Louis Cemetery Number 1. It is the "Holy Grail" of mausoleums, the burial site of the infamous Voodoo Queen, Marie Laveaux (Klein, 1962; Martinez, 1983).

By the time Marie was born, New Orleans was already established as a free black capital of the southern colonies where blacks and whites lived together in a multi-colored society. Marie's American ancestry began during the early 1700s with the colonization of Louisiana and the establishment of the city of La Nouvelle Orleans. Marie was born on September 16, 1801 as a free woman of color. Legend and folklore refer to her as born of a wealthy white planter, Charles Laveaux, and his beautiful half black–half Indian mistress, Marguerite. However, historical documents attest to the fact that her father was actually a free man of color, who was the son of the white French planter, Charles Laveaux Trudeau, the mayor of New Orleans in 1812. She was reported to have French, Native American, and African blood, and never once did she let anyone forget that she was proud of her ancestry. Her father spelled his chosen surname Laveaux and it this name she would have no doubt used had she been able to read and write. Unfortunately she could not, and archival records show her signature as a simple cross. Most people who are illiterate use an (X) to sign their names. However, Marie's use of the cross adds even more mystery and intrigue to her enigmatic personality. The cross symbolizes sacrifice, great deeds, compassion, and holiness. This was only one of the many facets of her character.

Although Marie's childhood was confined and confusing, the guidance of her grandmother Catherine was instrumental in influencing her self-esteem, confidence, and personal power, which would ultimately make her a legend in her own time. She grew into a beautiful woman of color, tall, statuesque, and regal. She bore a striking resemblance to her ancestors who were of African, White, and Native American descent. It was their spirits that no doubt guided and watched over her during her formative years.

She became a self-empowered free woman of color and was listed in New Orleans city directories as a Marchande; a woman who sold goods at the local French Marketplace alongside the Choctaw Indian women from the surrounding area.

Marie exhibited a unique combination of innate spiritual power, charismatic psychic abilities, astounding beauty, and a shrewd sense of business and politics. She was known locally and regionally for her generosity, compassion, and ministry to those in need, as well as her devotion to the Catholic Church.

To many people, Marie Laveaux was also known as a cunning fraud who used Voodoo as a way to a means. She has been depicted as a healer, sorceress, feminist, religious leader,

Voodoo Queen, and an anti-slavery activist, even though she was known to have bought slaves.

But who was this spirited woman, shrouded in mystery? The truth is as compelling as it is mysterious. Historical records, folklore, and urban legends have characterized Marie Laveaux as being beautiful, exotic, and sexually alluring. However, these physical descriptions can't begin to describe the combination of beauty, mystery, and charismatic energy that blended with her physical attributes to create all that she was, and all that she was destined to become.

In Africa the spoken word is believed to possess the magical power to create reality. Marie, being extremely talkative, was well aware of the power she possessed. Although French was her language of choice, she had mastered Creole English and several African and Native American languages. This gave her an advantage and added to her personal power to intervene in the lives of others.

She used the Catholic Church and the parish priest along with her Voodoo connections to influence the legal system and help the under-privileged and enslaved. Marie Laveaux exerted her female power in a patriarchal society. She expressed anger over the unfair distribution of power, wealth, and authority. She worked tirelessly to unite a scattered, confused, and abused people in order to restore their identities and sense of self-worth.

As a woman, she was able to tell fortunes, read palms, and gain the trust of both men and women who might be instrumental in helping her at some later date. She possessed a shrewd business sense, able to accumulate money and have enough to share with others in need.

Marie had a very private side as well. Although she gained notoriety by being married to a white man, she was a devoted wife, loving mother, caring grandmother, and supportive great-grandmother. As a devout Catholic, clairvoyant seer, and Voo-doo Queen, Marie Laveaux existed in several different realms of spiritual awareness.

First of all was her religious commitment to the Catho-lic Church, by attending daily mass at St. Louis Cathedral in New Orleans. Her benevolent spirit and charitable nature extended far beyond the church, outward into the city of New Orleans, rural parishes, Indian encampments, and the mysterious swamps of Louisiana. She ministered to her fam-ily, friends, and the downtrodden, as well as the wealthy, the enslaved, and imprisoned. She worked tirelessly as a "fever nurse," and was called upon by city officials to help during deadly cholera and yellow fever epidemics.

She was well known for taking in numerous abandoned street children. She fed and clothed them as well as educated them at times. Whenever she sponsored their education she relished in referring to them as her little protégées. Her small cottage was always full and she raised her own children as well as several of her grandchildren there. I think my own grandmother's favorite saying would certainly apply to Marie Laveaux; "If there is room in your heart, there is room in your house."

Her involvement in the slave market is just as well known, and perhaps even more intriguing. Although she provided

runaway slaves with charms to protect them on their journey north to freedom in Canada, and perhaps even helped
with the Underground Railroad, she played a bigger part in
her own benevolent way. Early Louisiana records attest to the
fact that she also bought and sold slaves. However, this was
not done as an investment, but rather as a way to liberate and
protect mothers and children from the bondage of slavery.
Whenever she made a purchase there was always a stipula-
tion that the slave gained their immediate freedom as a result
of the payment.

For over twenty years Marie Laveaux lent much of her
time and energy to the ministry of inmates who were on
death row in New Orleans' infamous Parish Prison.

She was allowed to visit the condemned prisoners as a spiritual guide and counselor. Serving in this capacity the prison
officials permitted her to erect altars for the inmates. She prepared and designed elaborate altars for the unfortunate men
awaiting execution. She draped each altar with crisp white
linen and added flowers, prayer books, and figurines of Catholic saints and angels.

On occasion the warden even allowed Marie to have a casket brought into the prison's cells. She helped the convicts
decorate it with images of the Voodoo religion and Catholic
iconology. One particular prisoner even slept in his own coffin for a few days before his execution.

By the 1830s she was working as a hairdresser to the
wealthy elite of New Orleans. She was always available to
visit them in their homes to help with their hair. By using her
expertise as a hairdresser she gained their trust and eventu-

ally became their personal confidant. This rapport gradually evolved into a more occult relationship where she foretold the future for them.

Her clients were among New Orleans' wealthiest upper-crust who could pay well for her services, and pay well they did. Some charms, spells, gris-gris, and medicinal cures could cost upwards of $1,000. She was highly sought after as a seer and served as advisor for many prominent white male officials. Many people came from hundreds of miles away to seek her advice and counsel. She used cards for divination as well as palm reading for additional insights into their lives, finances, and health issues. No doubt she used her innate gift of clairvoyance to compliment her wise counsel.

The force and effectiveness of her advice came from her mastery of vibrational frequencies and sincere spiritual awareness. However, one cannot discount her knowledge of the hidden affairs of New Orleans' judges, politicians, businessman, and wealthy white planters.

While working as a hairdresser she became privy to the private secrets of the rich and prosperous citizens of New Orleans. In her position as a clairvoyant seer she brought lovers together, removed hexes, and made gris-gris bags for good luck and to ward off evil when necessary. Her cures worked without fail and she helped her clients obtain relief from their psychological and physical sufferings.

Myths and legends began to surface about her amazing abilities. As she gained in notoriety she also maintained her extensive social network throughout the city. Through these connections and her innate wisdom she was able to circumvent many of the established laws that worked against women and slavery in Louisiana.

By the age of thirty-five, Marie Laveaux had become New Orleans' most powerful woman and Voodoo Queen. She had parlayed her knowledge of Louisiana politics, occult practices, clandestine secrets, and Voodooism into a force that overwhelmed most of the people she came into contact with. This force and ultimate power eventually propelled her into the role of Voodoo Queen.

After Marie Laveaux's retirement from her reign as Voodoo Queen at the 1872 Saint John's Eve celebration, she immediately withdrew to her home on Rue Saint Ann Street. She became a recluse for the last nine years of her life and refused to see any visitors or clients. She deferred all requests for Voodoo assistance to her oldest daughter Marie II, newly appointed Voodoo Queen.

The death of Marie Laveaux on June 15, 1881 was reported in many local and regional newspapers and even as far away as New York City. She was buried the next day with all the fanfare of Mardi Gras and the solemnity of the Roman Catholic Church, receiving full blessings and Catholic rites by the parish priest. Her funeral was attended by almost the entire population of New Orleans.

She was laid to rest at five o'clock in the afternoon. A late evening funeral assured that all blacks could attend. Marie's elaborate funeral procession, complete with cultural music, included blacks, whites, all of New Orleans' elite society, and men and women of all cultures and from all walks of life. There were so many people who came to pay their respects that one couldn't get within three blocks of St. Louis Cathedral. They stood in line, hats in hand, with their heads bowed, as they said their personal goodbyes to the Queen of New Orleans.

Marie Laveaux's death created one of the most notorious mysteries to ever grace the annals of old New Orleans. Today, Marie Laveaux still reigns in ghostly form over the mysterious world of Voodoo from St. Louis Cemetery. This remarkable woman, who faced down authority, defied rules, stood up to ridicule, and rebelled against racial harassment still wanders the streets of the French Quarter. This magnificent enchantress who charmed, healed, vexed, and supported a multicultural society remains secure in her aura of secrecy and mystique.

Even now her fame endures, as her legend continues to evolve and grow in popularity. Her old neighborhood in the French Quarter is rich with stories of visitations and sightings of the illustrious Voodoo Queen. Detailed accounts of a large black woman who strolls up and down the streets of New Orleans are plentiful. She frequently appears to unsuspecting visitors wearing her signature tignon.

The many ghost sightings of Marie Laveaux entitles New Orleans to its infamous reputation as the most haunted city in America. Her appearance as an ageless ghost in the French Quarter, in Congo Square, on the shore of Lake Pontchartrain, and of course in St. Louis Cemetery Number 1, happens with such consistency and regularity that there can be little doubt that she returns often to visit family, friends, and the city where she lived for almost a century.

Many Voodoo followers declare that Marie returns to life every year on St. John's Eve. She is often seen walking on the shore of Lake Pontchartrain where in life she presided over the festivities. In the Voodoo religion it is believed that when a Voodoo Queen dies her spirit reenters the river of life and moves to the next realm closest to this one. Her affinity for Lake Pontchartrain and the cleansing rituals performed there is probably the reason she appears there so often, especially on St. John's Eve.

Some of the most amazing ghost sightings involve Marie's ghost being seen in two places at the same time. In death, as in life, she possesses the occult ability to appear in different streets of New Orleans simultaneously; to tease, terrify, and perhaps welcome tourists to the surreal city. Many of the people who see her ghostly doppelganger are fascinated yet overwhelmed with fright.

New Orleans cemeteries are famous for their ghosts, and no one ghost excites more mystery, intrigue, and fear than Marie Laveaux. The most remarkable awe-inspiring visitations and manifestations of Marie Laveaux come from the French Quarter of New Orleans. Here Marie appears most often—always easily recognized by her cultural headwear, her white tignon.

Belief that Marie's spirit can be evoked to grant wishes eventually led to the naming of her burial mausoleum as the "Wishing Tomb." Tourists and locals flock to New Orleans to visit Marie Laveaux's mausoleum. Frightened, yet curious, they enter the surreal atmosphere of death—and life after death—as they approach her tomb.

Her Greek Revival tomb consists of three stacked crypts with a receiving vault (reciprocity for the remains of those displaced by new burials). Her three-tiered white stucco brick tomb is inscribed "Famille Veuve Paris née Laveau." A bronze plaque states that this is the burial place of Marie Laveaux the notorious Voodoo Queen. Mystery and intrigue surrounded her in life and have followed her to the grave. Not one day passes that someone, somewhere, doesn't mention her name, or Voodoo, her infamous claim to fame.

An estimated two hundred and fifty thousand people visit Marie's gravesite each year to carry out the ritual of three wishes. Historically three raps were made on the wall of her tomb to solicit her benevolent spirit. However, with the passage of time the three raps have been replaced with drawing three Xs in a row on the walls of her mausoleum. The cemetery personal have a steady job of washing down the walls to remove the Xs, but they always appear the next day, over and over, year after year, from one century to the next.

Drawing the three Xs originated with the African community of New Orleans. The X has long been an ancient African symbol denoting a crossroads between the realm of the living and the realm of spirit. To inscribe the three Xs is to symbolically call out to Marie Laveaux in a way she is sure to resonate to. And what better way to do so than in the cemetery, at the crossroads of mortality, to ensure that she will hear their requests and grant their wishes? The three Xs, when created and drawn with complete sincerity and concentrated desire assures that a Lwa will also intervene between the living and the spirit of Marie Laveaux.

Each mausoleum has its own personal energy and Marie Laveaux's is a fascinating example of the vibrational, magnetic energy that can be accessed either by knocking three times on the wall or drawing three Xs when a request is made. Her mausoleum is imbued with her charitable spirit, her charismatic Voodoo persona, and her soul's benevolent acceptance of all races and all cultures.

After a request for the three wishes is made, it is customary to leave Marie a small gift. These gifts are more often than not an assortment of things she would have enjoyed in life and will resonate to, such as flowers, rum, coins, food, and candy.

As the years pass Marie's magnificent mausoleum has withstood vandalism, hurricanes, and the ravages of time. It stands today as a monument and perhaps a testament to her immortality. Although it was her desire to slip away into the river of peace and contentment, she has been resurrected by a steady stream of friends, family, followers of Voodoo, tourists, and last but by no means least, a nationwide petition to grant everyone who comes to see her "Three Wishes." Paranormal investigators and ghost hunters all pursue Marie's ghost today, just as historians and writers have for over a century. Is Marie enticing them today as she has done in the past? She remains mysterious and alluring, yet also elusive. Visit New Orleans and catch a glimpse of the past. Perhaps Marie Laveaux, the notorious Voodoo Queen, will welcome you by showing up on your camera, or better yet, as a full manifestation of power and intrigue.

THE FLAMING TOMB

The Flaming Mausoleum was the burial place of New Orleans' infamous Storyville Madam, Josie Arlington (Klein, 1962; Taylor, 2003). Josie was born Mary Josephine Deubler to German parents in 1864. She changed her name over the years to suit her personality and further her career. In her early years of prostitution on the streets, she used the name Josie Alton. Later she changed it to Josie LoBrano, the name of her lover for several years. Finally after a vacation to Hot Springs, Arkansas where she fell in love with the famous Arlington Hotel, she changed her name once again to Josie Arlington. She kept this alias and would later name her infamous bordello The Arlington.

Orphaned at the tender age of four, she was taken in and raised by the nuns of St. Elizabeth's Home in New Orleans. Unfortunately their strict adherence to moral and religious tenets forced her adventurous spirit to rebel, and at the age of seventeen she turned to the streets in search of excitement and perhaps love.

She eventually met Philip LoBrano who took her in. He became her lover, as well as someone who would protect her as she pursued her life as a professional prostitute. From 1898 to 1917 an estimated three thousand prostitutes and madams lived and worked in the bordellos and brothels of New Orleans' red-light district known as Storyville.

A life of prostitution destroyed many women in New Orleans, but not Josie Arlington. As the years passed she gained a reputation as a tough, no-nonsense lady of the evening. However she knew that life as a prostitute could not last forever, especially as she aged and her beauty faded. She realized that to survive she would have to create a better way of life, even though in the same profession. She decided to take advantage of the men who had used her, and in order to do this she would have to become a madam. And this she accomplished, much to the astonishment of everyone who knew her.

She opened a bordello near the French Quarter. She purchased a four-story mansion with numerous bay windows, a tulip-domed cupola, fireplaces in every room, and according to Josie's extensive advertising "the works of great artists from Europe and America graced the walls." Despite her forceful personality and rowdy reputation her establishment was an elegant house where gentlemen paid high prices for her girls. Her bordello became very successful and the city of New Orleans was about to make her wealthier than she could ever imagine. Rather than fight overwhelming vices like prostitution and gambling, the city officials decided to control them by confining them to one supervised area; the district where Josie had opened her bordello.

Upper-class gentlemen, plantation owners, and business owners staggered through the streets, hypnotized by exotic drugs and liquor while being lured and seduced by scarlet ladies. Josie's bordello was beyond compare. It was the most lavish in the district. Beautiful women wearing the finest European lingerie lounged in the greeting parlor, waiting for the most powerful men in New Orleans, as well as wealthy men from other states and countries, to grace the doors of Josie's establishment.

While Josie enjoyed upper-class status within the boundaries of Storyville, she had a different reputation with New Orleans' high-society ladies. In an attempt to be accepted she bought a mansion in one of the city's most affluent neighborhoods, but she was still shunned and ignored by upper-class citizens of the port city.

As she grew older and her health began to fail she started to fixate on her mortality. Death, she decided, would allow her one last opportunity to get back at the society that abused her. She shocked New Orleans by purchasing a $2,000.00 plot in Metairie Cemetery, the most expensive and fashionable cemetery in all of New Orleans. The women who hated her and even the men who had enjoyed her services were mortified. They couldn't imagine a prostitute being buried among their loved ones, but there was nothing they could do.

Josie commissioned the eminent architect Albert Weiblen to create a magnificent mausoleum to her specifications. The mausoleum was large and ostentatious, costing more than $8,000.00. It was made of red granite and topped with two flambeaux. A statue of a young woman holding an armful of roses stands on the stairwell and appears to be knocking on the copper door that leads to Josie's final resting place.

After Josie was buried talk began to spread about strange things happening at her gravesite. People claim that they have seen the urns on top of the mausoleum burst into flames before their very eyes. Others have seen an eerie red glow coming from the tomb at night, as if the red granite walls were afire, and the symbolism of the red light coming from the mausoleum was certainly not lost on New Orleans high society.

Visitors to the gravesite have actually heard knocks as if the statue of the young lady was knocking to get in. Two gravediggers, Mr. Todkins and Mr. Anthony, have sworn that they saw the female statue walk away from her post and wander aimlessly among the graves before vanishing into thin air. They actually followed her on one occasion and watched as she simply disappeared again. Did they see the animated ghost of Josie Arlington? Does the statue embody her energy? I believe it is very possible. She possessed an amazing energy in life—why would she be any different in death?

As the stories spread, the cemetery became overrun with curiosity seekers wanting to see the strange events for themselves. Families of those buried in surrounding graves were horrified at the thought of their loved ones being trampled on. They demanded that Josie's remains be removed to an undisclosed location. Obviously money talks and Josie was disinterred and moved to an obscure vault inside the cemetery. Josie's mausoleum was then sold to someone else. Strangely enough the haunting phenomena have never ceased.

Although Josie may not have found the acceptance she craved in life, she has certainly gained notoriety in death.

TWELVE
PET CEMETERIES

When I was thinking about a chapter on pet cemeteries I couldn't help remembering the legends and folklore that I had heard repeatedly over the years about "Black Dogs." When I first became interested in ghost hunting the subject of black dogs would come up now and then, especially when we were conducting cemetery investigations. I always thought, o-k-a-y, and we should be scared why? It was just something that didn't seem important to me … then. Of course I was educated by seasoned investigators and today I am very appreciative of their patience while explaining this phenomenon to me.

As fate would have it—one day it happened! I actually saw a black dog while taking pictures in a rural graveyard. He just suddenly appeared from nowhere. One minute he wasn't there and then there he was across the cemetery walking among the tombstones. However, although he was much bigger than a Labrador retriever, he didn't have glowing red eyes and he didn't appear threatening. In fact he actually seemed oblivious to my presence in the graveyard.

Although I was admittedly a little anxious (no doubt because of all the stories I had heard), I *was* able to take a picture of it as I headed swiftly toward my truck. After I reached the safety of my truck I looked for the dog. He was nowhere to be seen. My perspective of black dogs was forever changed that day because as I reviewed my pictures what I saw was very disconcerting. Even though I had seen a big black dog, what appeared on my digital camera was a transparent, shadowy form of a dog.

Now that I had actually seen one I had to alter my beliefs and either accept or deny their presence, be it supernatural, ghostly, or some other weird presentation of energy such as a shape-shifter or an alien invader in disguise. Of course it is quite possible that they are dimensional creatures that appear and disappear through unseen portals, much the same as Bigfoot.

Throughout history the phenomenon of black dogs has appeared in legends, folklore, and numerous eyewitness accounts. Stories of black dogs are widespread and popular. This places them in a category all their own when it comes to paranormal phenomenon. These are primarily nocturnal sightings but have been sighted in broad daylight as well. They are regarded as omens of death for the person who sees them or for a close family member, especially if eye contact is made with them.

They are usually described as larger than the biggest breed of dogs and some have been reported to be as big as baby calves. They have an uncanny ability to appear and disappear into thin air in a matter of minutes. They have either red or yellow glowing eyes and seem at times to be leering at unsuspecting visitors in cemeteries and graveyards; almost as if displaying a sinister grin.

One would expect that with all these physical attributes you would hear noises associated with their presence; however, this is not the case. Reports of growling and barking are almost nonexistent. They seem content to simply project an evil persona, thereby terrifying the people who accidentally happen upon them.

Throughout recorded history they have been associated with electrical storms, crossroads, graveyards, and isolated roads. One particularly interesting account is that of a pack of black dogs with yellow eyes that are rumored to prowl U.S. Route 666 slashing the tires of passing motorists with their sharp teeth. This is interesting because of the paranormal history of Route 666, and the obvious ley line and portal activity generated in that area of Utah.

Sightings of black dogs are well documented in the folklore of almost every country and there is no doubt that people do encounter them occasionally. What their agenda may be is anyone's guess. I admit that I am puzzled by their ominous presence in graveyards. It has been six years since my spooky encounter in the isolated graveyard in Texas and I am still alive, but I didn't make eye contact with the dog.

Here's a bit of advice: always expect the unexpected, especially if you encounter a black dog on a dark night. As with any animal, wild or tame, you can never know for sure what their reaction will be at any given moment.

Many people, religions, and cultures as a whole believe that only humans possess a soul. These belief systems reject the fact that it is possible for animals to live on after death. They ignore (perhaps out of fear) the fact that animals do have souls and that after their deaths they can also choose to move on to eternal rest or stay behind to comfort their owners and loved ones in ghostly form.

Ghostly cats, dogs, horses, and birds are among the most commonly reported visitations, but any animal may appear as a full apparition or make contact by displaying any number of paranormal phenomena.

Most people will simply feel their pet's presence much the same way that we sense our family and friends who have transcended death. We may feel them brush against us, feel a damp nose nuzzle our hands, and many of us actually see our pets as they curl up next to us on our beds.

While this is startling, it can also be very comforting. Our pets offer us unconditional love, protection, and attention. Who among us would not be happy to receive this gift of eternal love and devotion from the other side?

Auditory experiences are also common and typically involve a person hearing their pets make noises much as they did while they were alive. They may hear the sound of scratching at the door, barks, meows, and other sounds associated with feeding times. It's not uncommon at all to hear paws scamper across the floor and barking when there is a knock at the door. Like the ghosts of humans, our pets seem to haunt or visit places where they lived, played, or even worked.

Many animals pass from this lifetime to the next vibrational dimension without much fanfare. Sadly they are often abandoned, euthanized, or neglected at the time of their demise. However, just as many pets are loved and nurtured throughout their lives and as they lay dying.

After our beloved pets die comes the decision of burial or disposal of their bodies. For devoted pet owners this can sometimes become a very traumatic undertaking. The places of interment are as varied as the pet owners themselves. Pets have been found entombed with Egyptian pharaohs, interred in cemeteries created just for them, and buried in secluded out-of-the-way sites for generations. Just think of how many little goldfish, turtles, frogs, hamsters, and birds are buried in backyards, and rose gardens across America today. Swimming, flying, creeping, and crawling—they reach their final destinations of eternal rest. But what if they aren't ready to go? Do they return to flutter about the house or splash in water that no one sees?

The same goes for larger pets: dogs and horses, for instance. Some of America's most legendary haunted cemeteries are visited by the ghosts of dogs, cats, and other animals that were pets or were domesticated to work and labor on farms, in circuses, rodeos, and a multitude of other occupations.

Today haunted pet cemeteries are hosts to many paranormal investigators and ghost hunters. My guess is that one reason they are so eagerly sought out is that there aren't the same fears that are attached to ghostly human cemeteries and graveyards. Most people love animals and animals love them back, so fear is less of an issue, especially in the dark of night.

However, just because these pets are laid to rest doesn't necessarily mean that they will remain thus forever. They can and do return to lovingly caress their previous owners and in some cases interact with visitors and mourners in pet cemeteries.

The following stories demonstrate this fact and may help you relate to animal ghosts, and even ease the grieving process for some readers.

JIM THE WONDER DOG

Marshall Ridge Cemetery is a beautiful retreat surrounded by nicely manicured lawns and old brick buildings. Within these serene surroundings rests the gravesite of a very unique dog, "Jim the Wonder Dog" (Mitchell, 1942).

Jim was a surprisingly gifted Llewellyn setter who died in 1937. Although it's unusual for a park to be named in memory of someone's pet, in 1999 the town of Marshall dedicated Jim the Wonder Dog Memorial Park to this mystical dog. The park located in the middle of town offers a peaceful respite for visitors and townsfolk alike. A large statue of Jim guards the entrance and winding walkways take visitors past a gazebo and over a small brook. Plaques are stationed along the way that describe Jim's amazing life and accomplishments. Gazing on his beautiful soul effigy, one can almost feel his presence. Indeed many visitors and passersby are rumored to have seen Jim romping through the cemetery at twilight and in the early morning hours of dawn. Just as many stories abound regarding people who have received inspiring messages and guidance while standing at his gravesite.

Jim, a gentle and intelligent setter, was born on March 3, 1925, at the Taylor Kennels in Louisiana. He was eventually purchased by Samuel VanArsdale who operated the Ruff Hotel in Marshall, Missouri.

Llewellyn setters are very friendly. They are also mild-mannered, sensitive, and enthusiastic, so perhaps one shouldn't be surprised that these peaceful, graceful dogs could also display remarkable mystical abilities such as telepathy, precognition, and intuition. These unique setters are a very specific pure strain of English setters that have bloodlines tracing back to the breeding programs of Purcell Llewellyn and Edward Laverack during the early 1900s.

Until Jim was three years old he enjoyed his life as a normal hunting dog. Then rather unexpectedly one day his owner noticed that Jim was obeying his commands as if he could really understand the English language. During one particular hunting trip, Jim's owner, Sam VanArsdale, unconsciously murmured out loud that he was going to rest beneath a nearby hickory tree. Immediately Jim went to the exact hickory tree and sat down. VanArsdale was intrigued by his actions and began to name tree after tree, one variety after another and each time Jim would go directly to the tree Sam had named and place his paws on it.

VanArsdale was amazed and started giving informal demonstrations of Jim's power to friends, family, and neighbors. He would tell Jim to go to a particular person wearing certain color clothing, and without fail Jim successfully repeated the exercises over and over again.

He would also tell Jim to find an automobile with certain letters and numbers on the license plate. Once again Jim was able to accomplish this without making mistakes. Jim found the car every single time.

Word spread quickly. VanArsdale and his incredible setter were asked to come before a combined session of the local lawmakers in Jefferson City, Missouri where a test had been devised to debunk the setter's uncanny abilities.

In order to preclude any secret signaling by VanArsdale, commands were tapped out in Morse code telling Jim to walk over to certain members in the room. To everyone's amazement Jim did it! The senators and representatives sat in awe of Jim as he picked out people by their body type, distinguishing marks, personality traits, and hair color.

His talents and notoriety reached an apex after he developed or refined his innate ability to predict future events. He could foretell the sex of unborn children, the winner of the World Series and presidential elections, and even the winners of seven consecutive Kentucky Derbies. He was so skilled at predicting race winners that his owner had to cut short a vacation because of a telegram threatening Jim's life if he didn't stop picking winners at the dog races. VanArsdale was obviously very upset and concerned that someone would attempt to steal or worse yet, harm his beloved pet.

Because of this he turned down a very profitable offer from Paramount Studios as well as other lucrative offers from dog food companies. VanArsdale was adamant that Jim not be exposed to the public and said "I feel that Jim's powers are beyond my comprehension and I do not care to commercialize on them in any way!"

Jim died on March 18, 1937, having lived out his lifespan; he was twelve years old. The VanArsdales asked to be allowed to bury Jim in Marshall Ridge Cemetery. However, the cemetery sexton would only agree to a burial just outside the fence. Interestingly enough over the years the cemetery expanded and actually took in Jim's gravesite, thereby granting the VanArsdales their wish after all.

Do our pets possess innate psychic abilities that allow them to tune into other dimensions, their owners, and even see into the future? And if purebred Llewellyn setters are endowed with the gifts of intuition, telepathy, clairvoyance, and clairaudience, wouldn't you want one for a pet?

KABAR

Hidden away among the gently rolling hills of Calabasas, California are ten beautifully landscaped acres that encompass the Los Angeles Memorial Pet Cemetery. The cemetery provides a tranquil setting for the gravesites of some of Hollywood's most famous pets as well as thousands of other animals.

The cemetery was founded in 1928, and rapidly became the chosen cemetery for burials of the beloved and adored pets of the rich and famous. Petey, the pit bulldog who enjoyed his role as playmate to the Little Rascals was laid to rest here. Also buried in the cemetery is Topper, Hopalong Cassidy's famous horse.

However, it is the gravesite of Rudolph Valentino's dog, Kabar, that attracts the most attention. Kabar, who died in 1929, was a gentle giant; a harlequin Great Dane. Valentino loved horses and dogs, and Kabar was a loyal, devoted companion. Great Danes are regal dogs that combine nobility with power and elegance. Kabar was a fitting pet for the man who became the most famous heartthrob to ever grace the Silver Screen (Rule, 2001).

Great Danes are overwhelmingly friendly, so it should come as no surprise that Kabar would enjoy greeting visitors to the cemetery, even in ghostly form. Visitors to Kabar's gravesite frequently report that they have heard barks and panting sounds. However, it is the playful licks that he gives visitors that affirm his ghostly presence.

One might easily pass off hearing barking noises and sounds of a panting dog to an over active imagination. But, a big, wet, lapping lick from a Great Dane would be a spine-tingling event. One that couldn't be explained any other way than as paranormal phenomenon generated by a gentle giant ... Kabar.

NIGHT-LIFE

Clara-Glen Pet Cemetery, which opened in 1918, is located in Linwood, New Jersey, outside Atlantic City. In 1959 the *Ocean City Sentinel* printed an article describing one of the largest funerals ever held in Atlantic City. This was not an uncommon event—however, the deceased was. The funeral was held for a local bartender's dog named Night-Life. Night-Life belonged to Spanky Davis and was of rather questionable back street pedigree (www.weirdnj.com).

Night-Life was well known by everyone and had a peculiar way with people who were intoxicated. Whenever he saw a tipsy customer on the street he would guide them out of harm's way. He was also known to hail cabs, and all the cabbies would stop when they saw him standing on the street corner. They would either give a ride to his inebriated friends or just give him a ride for fun, enjoying his company as well. When Night-Life died a collection was taken up to bury him. He was laid to rest in a white, satin-lined coffin.

People from far and wide came to pay their respects to Night-Life as they filed past his casket to say their final goodbyes. His funeral procession was respectful and lengthy, and there were twenty limousines in the line of cars behind the hearse. Six pallbearers attended the coffin and an Atlantic City newspaper publisher came to read his eulogy.

Sometimes, late at night, people will see a dog standing on the street corner where Night-Life used to hail cabs, and then he will just disappear. Does he return to check on his friends and customers?

THIRTEEN
ROADSIDE
MEMORIALS

Who among us has not seen a white cross on the side of the road, nailed to a tree, or erected at an isolated intersection? And who among us has not slowed down to pay our respects for the person or persons who lost their lives at that very spot?

Have you ever wondered what mystery lies behind the growing number of crosses appearing along our roadways? These small roadside memorials have become sacred spaces to the loved ones of the people who died at the site of the cross.

I used to be puzzled about the spiritual significance of roadside crosses. Having never lost anyone to a fatal accident I was at a loss to understand why the place of death held a stronger spiritual connection with an individual than the place where their loved ones were buried.

More and more people are now exerting their rights to set up roadside memorials that function outside the confines of traditional religion and outside the boundaries of cemeteries and graveyards.

What force or mysterious expressions of spirituality guides them to connect with their loved ones in this manner? The obvious answer is that very powerful energies exist at the site of a tragic death, and this energy can be tapped into for communication.

Although death may have freed the person from their physical bodies, the sudden shock of an untimely death may have made a peaceful, full transition impossible. They may still be able to communicate with their loved ones according to their intent and desire to facilitate emotional healing.

While extremely heartbreaking for loved ones who erect the memorial crosses, they are unknowingly seeking that energy connection. In doing so, they unconsciously set up energy memorials that could at times open spiritual portals allowing communication to take place to ease the pain and suffering of grief. Memorializing someone helps with the grieving process. Perhaps no one was more aware of this custom than Native Americans. Historically and traditionally they sanctify the ground where a death takes place. It becomes holy ground and should be respected.

Do ghosts remain at the scene of the accident? Could this be the reason for so many accounts of mysterious phantom hitchhikers and unusual sightings on the side of roadways across America?

A young woman from Tennessee had a startling experience regarding a simple roadside cross. Her story may help shed some light on ghost sightings at the sites of fatal highway accidents (www.blogarea51.org).

While going to college in central Tennessee she delivered pizza at night for extra money. There were a lot of wooded areas near the college and some of the orders she received carried her down nearby rural roads.

On one particular night, close to midnight, she received a call from a man who lived just outside of town. It wasn't unusual to get calls that late because the pizza parlor stayed open until 2 a.m. to accommodate the college students.

She was prepared to deliver the pizza, but not for what she experienced on the isolated dark road. As she was driving along she noticed that her headlights beamed across a small white cross on the side of the road. It was draped in flowers and stood as a testament to a tragic accident.

Her attention was captured not by the cross itself, but by a thick fog that appeared to be coming from beneath it. The mist rose upward and above the small white cross. As she drove on past the cross she experienced only a mild curiosity about the odd occurrence she had witnessed.

However, a second call from the same man on the second night gave her cause to feel a little uncomfortable. Although it wasn't unusual to have repeat customers, this man didn't live at a dorm or in a local neighborhood.

On her second trip she was looking for the little white cross and to her surprise there appeared to be a column of fog at the cross that looked suspiciously like the loose shape of a person. Although not as clear, it did have a faint human outline. Thinking that perhaps her mind must be playing tricks on her she drove on to deliver the pizza.

The new customer ordered a pizza every night for a week. And every night that she passed the cross the misty figure became more defined. The last night was a Sunday and she felt that someone else should take the delivery, because now she was feeling very anxious about the delivery and what she was seeing as she passed the roadside memorial. However, as fate would have it someone called in sick and she was forced to make the delivery once again. As she approached the memorial she could see the dense, well defined figure of a young girl standing behind the cross. By the time she arrived at the house to deliver the pizza, she was totally shaken and very upset.

As she handed the man his pizza she asked him if he had any idea what had happened back down the road where the little white cross stood. What he told her only added to her nervous confusion.

Much to her astonishment he told her that his daughter had died there in an automobile accident a year earlier! Shocked and clearly shaken she left the house overwhelmed with emotion. This experience has stayed with her for many years and she will never forget the ghost of the young girl that appeared at the little white cross; the place of her untimely death.

The man never ordered another pizza again. Perhaps he was profoundly affected by her story and her reaction to his daughter's death. Or perhaps he realized that his daughter had found a way to communicate from beyond the grave and was overwhelmed with this knowledge. Either way she was able to manifest her energy through sheer intent and desire in an attempt to communicate.

FIVE CROSSES

When I first began this chapter on roadside memorials I had the good fortune to meet someone very special. This story may forever change the way you look at death and dying, as well as the way you view the little white crosses we all see everyday as we travel the roadways of America.

The following is an account of R. J. "Cowboy" Carter's remarkable, unforgettable experience with the paranormal (www.boozefighters21.com).

R. J. awoke early one morning to find a long honey-do list that his wife had left for him. Although not one to avoid his chores, for some inexplicable reason he was drawn to his motorcycle. Chores or a bike ride, which would it be? The bike ride won out and he began his mysterious journey into the realm of paranormal events.

The road in front of his house runs straight into some of the Sierras' prime motorcycle-riding country and he had heard a lot of good things about an old saloon up on Highway 88. He decided to visit the saloon for a cheeseburger and cocktail. He soon reached scenic Jenkinson Lake and the turn off to the Old Mormon Immigrant Trail Road that led to Highway 88 and the old saloon.

As he road his bike a strange sequence of events began to unfold. While calmly cruising along at about 45 mph and taking in all the wonders of an early morning in the Sierras, he became so immersed in his thoughts that he actually forgot where he was.

Suddenly, on a perfectly smooth, well-paved road, he slammed into a rock the size of a bowling ball. He immediately pulled over to check for damages to his bike, and found that it wasn't too bad, just a slightly bent rim. However, as he stood there surveying his damaged bike, an eerie feeling that he was being watched overwhelmed him. He looked up and noticed on the hillside a row of five white crosses. These crosses weren't on the roadside as most often seen, but above the road about fifteen feet up on the edge of a tall embankment.

Large and uniform, the crosses loomed over him like an unearthly beacon or ghostly testimonial. He knew that somehow, some way, he had been brought to this exact spot for a reason. He realized he wasn't there by mere chance.

Whether because of an innate curiosity or a spiritual direction, he began clawing and scratching his way up the side of the embankment. Grabbing pine trees while cussing and swearing, he painfully came to the realization that there wasn't anything in the forest that doesn't sting you, stick you, or bite you.

Weary and bruised from the climb, R. J. finally made his way to the top and steadied himself by clutching one of the large white crosses. It was then that he saw behind the crosses a small clearing containing an eerie sight.

Perched on top of a large concrete pedestal was a burned-up motor of a Harley Davidson, with a large plaque attached to it that read: *"This marks one of the worst tragedies in motorcycle history. The purpose of this memorial is to never forget those of us who have fallen, and to remind us of how precious life is and how quickly it can be taken away. Live to ride, ride to live, God speed and please be careful."*

Apparently, many riders who had visited the site left something as a remembrance. The entire memorial was covered and lovingly adorned with relics, mementoes, knick-knacks, and other offerings in honor of the fallen riders. Even the crosses themselves were draped with bandanas, key chains, and flowers from recent visitors to the shrine.

As he stood there in the deafening silence he was overwhelmed with the peace and tranquility of the site. All the time he was there not one car or truck passed on the busy road below, there was no noise to interrupt him from paying homage to his newfound friends. Friends he never would have had a chance to meet if not for their deaths.

No worse for wear, he stumbled back down the hill and made it back to his bike. He quickly decided that his initial destination, the old saloon, might as well be on the dark side of the moon, and he headed for home.

However, a couple of miles down the road he began to experience an emotional, overpowering feeling that he had unfinished business or had forgotten something back at the memorial.

So he instantly answered the call of the supernatural, turned his chopper around, bent rim and all, and headed back to the site. It was almost as if someone was telling him, "Hey get back up here, you missed something!"

But what could he have missed, he wondered. What else was there? Then he noticed a narrow road that he hadn't seen before, off to the right amid the trees just as he got to the site where the horrible accident had happened.

Unable to stop the flow of events, he followed the trail all the way up to the monument. He didn't need to climb the side of the hill after all. There in front of him was at least fifty yards of level walkway that led all the way to the top of the hill where the crosses stood. Groomed and well-maintained, it made an easy walk for all visitors. It became increasingly obvious that someone or something had called him back to this spot to show him what he had missed before, and what they desperately needed for him to see.

After that R. J. went on to the office of the *Mountain Demo-crat*, the local newspaper in town, to find out more about the accident. Since it had been almost seventeen years earlier, the newspaper referred him to the county library, where after a mile or so of microfilm he found the story.

It was the worst accident in El Dorado County history. The firefighters and emergency medical personnel who responded to the accident initially thought there were two dead bikers, along with a truck that had caught fire. As they started putting out the fire, they started finding more and more motorcycle parts, and more and more bodies. So gruesome was the scene that all the service personnel had to attend psychiatric sessions as a means of evaluating trauma induced by the grim tragedy.

The initial reports of the accident, which occurred five miles east of Sly Park Road on Saturday, September 2, 1989, were also incorrect, stating that the bikes had inadvertently just hit some wood in the road. An extensive investigation by the California Highway Patrol found that a one-ton flatbed truck filled with firewood was westbound on Mormon Immigrant Trail. A group of about thirty-five motorcyclists were riding two-abreast in the eastbound lane on their way to the annual Hope Valley Run. For unknown reasons the truck lost control on a straight stretch of road. The truck traveled off to the right side of the road, then apparently overcorrected and careened back across the westbound lane. When the truck entered the eastbound lane the first two motorcycles in the formation struck the truck broadside. The truck then overturned directly into four of the cycles, crushing them and their riders. At the same time the large load of firewood spilled out onto the roadway forcing four more motorcycles to go down. Meanwhile the truck caught fire, apparently due to a ruptured gas tank on the bikes or the truck itself, sending out a wall of flame engulfing everything. Dead at the scene were Douglas Wall, twenty-four, of Reno; Jeffrey Pearl, forty-one, of Foster City; Deborah Sund, twenty-three, and her husband Jeffrey Sund, thirty-one, of Carmichael; along with James Carter, thirty-five, of Sacramento.

What if anything makes this a strange story? When R. J. reviewed the chain of events: choosing to neglect his chores just to take a bike ride, even taking his camera along just have a cheeseburger, it seemed odder still. After thirty years of riding bikes, how could he not have seen, much less hit, a large rock that seemed to appear out of nowhere at the exact spot where the tragic accident took place? What happened to set these events in motion?

What R. J. didn't reveal at first was that one single cross stood out from all the rest, and caught his attention. It wasn't because the cross was any different from the others, but it was the only one that was glowing brightly through the dense forest, illuminated by a single ray of sunlight cast directly on it.

Because the cross was glowing so brightly he singled it out, and began his frantic climb up the hill toward it. When he reached the cross and clutched it with his hand, he read the inscription; "James Carter"! As he read the name everything fell into place and it became perfectly clear to him: why he was there, who had brought him to the site, the rock in the road, everything. He realized that he wasn't there by chance. He was summoned by James Carter to tell the story.

Like his father, whose name had been James Carter, his name is also James Carter, the inscription on the cross. What are the odds? Spooky fate or creepy coincidence, either way there is more to the story.

R. J. is adamant about the fact that anyone who has ever been to the site will know what he means when he says Jeff, Deborah, Doug, Jeffrey, and James are all still there. You can feel them standing next to you in the gentle mountain breeze. You can hear them speak to you through your heart. All they ask is to please never forget how precious life is, and how quickly it can be taken away, and that someday if you have the chance they would like you to come up, visit, and take the time to reflect and make some new friends.

This amazing story does not end here. Not long after Cowboy Carter published this article on his website, he received correspondence from a young man named Josh Adams Carter. He thanked R. J. Carter for writing the article and told him how much it meant to him. You see, R. J. Carter had written about a man Josh had never gotten to meet: his father, James Carter! Through circumstances beyond his control he had been estranged from his father's family. His mother had remarried and he was adopted by his mother's second husband. He had never met anyone from his father's side of the family until he read R. J. Carter's article. Now years later he was able to find members of his father's family and reestablish family ties. All of this was made possible by the ghostly communication between him and his father, James Carter, who was killed in that fateful motorcycle accident.

This amazing story is remarkable in that it reunited a father with his son through death. It proves beyond a shadow of a doubt that there is no death and we do not die. As for Cowboy Carter's reaction to this amazing paranormal event and the part he played in it, he said: "I've never been a true believer in the paranormal, so that day for me was like coming face to face with a Great White Shark in deep water. I know now that there is something more out there!"

FOURTEEN
CEMETERY EPITAPHS

In early America it wasn't necessarily the shape of the tombstone or the material it was carved from that caught mourners off-guard. It was the unusual and sometimes cryptic or even witty epitaphs that caused visitors to stop and reflect on their own mortality.

As a ghost-hunter I have read countless tombstone inscriptions and epitaphs. Many are witty, some are weird, but most are spiritual and may even tug at your heart strings. I began copying those that interested me most, and soon had added many different inscriptions to my files. Many were collected on personal visits to cemeteries, some were found as I researched ghosts and paranormal phenomena, and just as many were given to me by other investigators and friends. I have included some of them in this chapter.

When tombstones first appeared in churchyards they were erected primarily to honor the deceased, or perhaps appease evil spirits. As more and more people used tombstones to engrave their epitaphs on they became a popular way to identify the deceased, tell about their lives, their work, and at times the cause of their untimely deaths.

Tombstones usually bear inscriptions of the deceased's name and dates of birth and death. However, they may also reflect how the deceased wishes to be remembered. Epitaphs offer a final chance to say goobye or leave a message for family and friends, if chosen by the deceased. If not, then fortunately, or in many cases unfortunately, the deceased is memorialized by a member of the family, who may, or may not, be sweet spirited toward the deceased. This very situation has created some extremely interesting, cryptic, witty, and mysterious epitaphs.

The message may be religious, or a testament to one's faith. They may also be humorous, philosophical, or inscribed with thought-provoking messages. Of course, they can also reflect the darker side of human nature and be inscribed to confuse, hide a secret message, or even reveal an occult life. It's not uncommon to see an epitaph in the form of a curse, or an admonishment for society as a whole. William Shakespeare's epithet is a good example.

Good Friend, for Jesus sake forebear,
To dig dust enclosed here.
Blest be to the man that spares these stones,
And cursed be he that moves my bones.

Our graveyards and cemeteries are invaluable and distinctive treasures. They contain a rich and relatively untapped source of funerary art, as well as a wealth of genealogical information for future generations to access.

Memorial epitaphs, embellishments, and inscriptions record the frailty of human life. They can also reveal how generations before us lived and died, their religious beliefs, how they felt about death and dying, and their superstitions regarding ghosts and spirits.

Writers in the 1600s suggested that an epitaph should consist of the name, the age, the deserts, the dignities, and their state, the praise both of body and mind, and the manner and time of the death. As an astrologer I wish they would have followed through with this data. What a revealing aspect of the epitaph this would have been. To see someone's time of birth, or better yet, their astrology chart etched on their tombstone would be the ultimate reward for me after spending so many hours pursuing ghost and occult mysteries.

Seventeenth-century epitaphs were usually brief and factual, but in the eighteenth and nineteenth centuries they became increasingly more artistic, descriptive, ridiculous, and often cryptic or witty.

Longevity was a rare thing and was frequently inscribed on archaic tombstones. Here are some pretty remarkable examples found throughout Europe.

TOMBSTONE TESTIMONIES

At Bolton-on-Swale a few miles from Northalerton, Yorkshire; a churchyard tomb commemorates a man who had lived to an incredible age.

Henry Jenkins—169 years old
Born 1501–Died 1670

In the churchyard of St. Luke's in Bristington, Bristol, the epitaph of Thomas Newman reads:

1542 Thomas Newman aged 153

This stone was refaced in 1771 to preserve the validity of the incredible age of the deceased.

In Great Willaston, Cheshire is the epitaph of Thomas Parr who died in Shropshire in 1635 at the age of 152 and was buried in Westminster Abbey.

Thomas Damme, a native of Chester, Died at the age of 154.

Issac Ingall, butler of Battle Abbey in Sussex, reached a mere 120 years of age.

Stoke-on-Trent churchyard has the tombstones of Henry and Sibil Clarke, who both died in 1684; and both at the age of 112.

This is the epitaph of Matthew Peat at Wirksworth, Derbyshire, who died at the age of 112. He has an interesting epitaph, however contradictory.

Few lives so long;
Who lives well?

Sarah Jarvis of Corsham, Wiltshire died in 1753 at the age of 107. Her epitaph reads:

She had sometime before her death; a third set of teeth.

Epitaph of William Billinge.
William Billinge of Longnor, Staffordshire was born in a cornfield, served at Gibraltar and died in 1791 at the age of 112.

Joseph Watson, keeper of a deer park, was buried at Disley, Cheshire. He lived to be 104 years old.

Ammie Abraham of Kilmersder, Somerset; her tombstone epitaph stated that until two years before her death in 1849 she walked regularly to her work, a distance of one and a half miles every day. She died at the age of 104.

Perhaps these epitaphs have brought peace and comfort to those who fear death and a short existence and perhaps they will give many people hope, in a time when death was often premature.

Epitaphs grow more interesting with each new generation. Here are some that I found interesting, hope you will too.

Wyatt Earp
There's nothing so sacred as honor and nothing so loyal
as love.

——

Here lies Ann Mann
Who lived an Old Maid
But died an Old Mann
Dec. 8, 1767.

——

Here lies
Johnny Yeast
Pardon me
For not Rising.

——

Here lies the body
Of Jonathan Blake
Stepped on the gas
Instead of the brake.

——

Here lays Butch
We planted him raw
He was quick on the trigger
But slow on the draw.

——

Sacred to the memory of
My husband John Barnes

Who died January 3, 1803
His comely young widow, aged 23, has many qualifications
of a good wife, and yearns to be "comforted"!

———

Here lies Ezekiel Aikle
Age 102
The good Die Young

———

Sir John Strange
Here lies an honest lawyer
And that is strange.

———

Here lies Lester Moore
Four slugs from a .44
No Les, No More.

———

On the 22nd of June
Jonathan Fiddle
Went out of tune.

———

Here lies the body of our Anna
Done to death by a banana
It wasn't the fruit that laid her low
But the skin of the thing that made her go.

———

Gone away
Owing more
Than he could pay.

In memory of Beza Wood
Departed this life
Nov. 2, 1827 aged 45 years
Here lies one Wood—Enclosed in Wood
One Wood, within another
The outer Wood—Is very good
We cannot praise, The other.

Under the sod and under the trees
Lies the body of Jonathan Pease
He is not here, there's only the pod;
Pease shelled out and went to God.

The grave of Ellen Shannon
Who was fatally burned
March 21, 1870
By the explosion of a lamp
Filled with "R. E. Danforth's
Non-explosive Burning Fluid.

Harry Edsel Smith
Looked up the elevator shaft to see
if the car was on the way down; it was!

Here lies an Atheist
All dressed up
And no place to go.

———

John Dryden, (1631–1700) for his wife:
Here lies my wife; here let her lie!
Now she's at rest, and so am I!

———

Here lies all that remains of Charlotte
Born a virgin, died a harlot
For sixteen years she kept her virginity
A marvelous thing for this vicinity.

———

Effie Jean Robinson (1897–1922)
Come blooming youths, as you pass by
And on these lines do cast an eye,
As I am now, so must you be
Prepare for death and follow me,
(Underneath someone had added:
To follow you, I am not content
How do I know, which way you went!)

———

He was young
He was fair
But the injuns
Raised his hair.

———

Bill Blake
Was hanged by Mistake.

————

Here lies a man named Zeke
Second fastest draw in Cripple Creek.

————

Here lies the body of
Thomas Kemp
Who lived by wool
And died by Hemp.

————

Here lies the body
Of Margaret Bent
She kicked up her heels
And away she went.

————

Rebecca Freeland—1741
She drank good Ale,
Good punch, and Wine
And lived to the age of 99!

————

1690—Here lie the bones of Joseph Jones
Who ate while he was able.
But once over fed, he dropped down dead
And fell beneath the table.
When from the tomb, to meet his doom,

He arises amidst sinners,
Since he must dwell in Heaven or Hell
take him—whichever gives the best dinners.

———

On the stone of a grave digger:
Hooray my brave boys
Let's rejoice at his fall
For if he had lived
He would have buried us all.

———

Here lies Robert Trollope (an architect)
Who made stones tall up
When death took his soul up
His body filled this hole up.

———

Stranger tread
This ground with gravity
Dentist Brown
Is filling his last cavity.

———

Jebediah Goodwin (auctioneer)
Born 1828
Going !
Going !!
Gone !!!
1876.

———

1787 Jones 1855
Here lies the bones of Sophie Jones;
For her death held no tears
She was born a maid and died a maid
No hits, no runs, and no heirs.

———

Here lies the father of 29
Who would have had more
But he didn't have time.

———

Grieve not for me my husband dear.
I am not dead but sleeping here.
With patience wait—perforce to die
And in a short time you'll come to I.
And her husband added
I am not grieved, my dearest wife,
Sleep on, I've got another wife.
Therefore, I cannot come to thee
For I must go and live with she.

———

I plant these shrubs upon your grave, dear wife,
That something in this spot may boast of life.
Shrubs must wither and all earth must rot
Shrubs may revive, but you thank Heaven will not.

———

1796—Wise—1878
Here lies the body of Ephraim Wise

Safely tucked between his two wives
One was Tillie, and the other Sue
Both were faithful, loyal, and true
By his request in ground that's hilly
His coffin is set tilted toward Tillie.

————

Tears cannot restore her
Therefore I weep!

————

Here beneath this stone we lie
Back to back my wife and I
And when the angel's trump shall thrill
If she gets up then I'll lie still.

————

Here lies Elizabeth
My wife for 47 years
And this is the first damn thing
She ever did to oblige me.

————

Atheist author Haine's epitaph:
Haine
Haint!

————

Here lies the body of Mary Ann Lowder
She burst while drinking a Seidlitz powder
Called from this world to her heavenly rest
She should have worked till it effervescened.

Blown upward
Out of sight
He sought the leak
By candlelight!

———

If you could choose your own epitaph, what would you say? I have spent a lot of time in cemeteries over the years, first out of curiosity, then as a mourner. More recently as a ghost hunter and photographer. I wandered aimlessly up and down the spirit-filled pathways of the deceased seeking closure, assurance, and wisdom. I often asked myself what, if anything, would I want to say to family and friends as my body lay still and my soul soared to new heights of awareness.

It was then that my personal belief and adherence to the tenets of Spiritualism begged to be acknowledged, as did my sincere belief in Reincarnation and Life after Death. As these three beliefs remove the boundaries of time and space, they allow us to not only remember and be remembered, but to also see, feel, and be heard beyond the grave for all eternity. With this in mind I decided on my epitaph.

There is no Death and we do not Die!
****

From this lifetime to the next,
This is true,
My soul will always remember you.

I hope that these epitaphs have given you a few laughs as well as food for thought. Have you decided what you want on your tombstone, before someone else chooses for you?

FIFTEEN
RESEARCHING
CEMETERY
MYSTERIES

Ghost hunting is exciting and intriguing, but it also involves dedication, perseverance, and research. Conducting investigative research into cemeteries and graveyards is much the same as researching a building or someone's residence. The same rules apply. As we investigate paranormal phenomena we want to know more about the people who are buried in the cemeteries we visit, and of course the ghosts who reside there as well.

In a sense we become detectives as we explore secrets from the past. We also learn more about ourselves during the process. As we explore death and cemeteries, we may find ourselves changing our viewpoints and deeply rooted beliefs that define our own spirituality.

Eventually our research leads us to haunted cemeteries. We read tombstones and headstones, seeking answers to ghostly questions. As ghost hunters venture into one cemetery after another they become more familiar with tombstones, monuments, and headstones inscribed with unique artistic designs and personal symbolism.

Questions will usually arise about the meanings of the designs and symbols and even mysterious cryptic messages that are often found on tombstones and markers. Can interpreting these symbolic images help us discover more about the deceased, their lifestyles, professions, organizations, and perhaps even their hobbies? Yes they can.

When researching cemeteries and graveyards it may become necessary to decipher the universal, regional, and cultural meanings of tombstone art in order to uncover more about the deceased. These beautiful archaic designs and symbols usually have specific meanings and will add valuable information to investigations as well as solving cemetery mysteries.

Most of the symbols you see etched or engraved on tombstones will probably have been engraved because someone just liked them, or they were a favorite of the deceased. In this sense they will have little meaning beyond the personal preference of the deceased or the living that are left behind to purchase the tombstone or defining marker and make the final arrangements for everlasting repose.

Most of the people who choose tombstone designs or personal artistic representations actually have no idea of the meaning of the symbols; they probably chose the symbol because they liked the floral design, artistic ornamentation, or something that reminded them of their deceased love ones. Often family members will select something that will evoke everlasting memories for future generations.

This soon becomes an integral part of ghost hunting. The placement of the grave itself can sometimes tell us as much as the information on the tombstone or its epitaph. Tombstones and monuments will provide a tremendous amount of information about those who are interred there. You may also be able to discover additional information about the cemetery while you are on an investigation.

For me, the key to understanding who is buried in a cemetery and why is the cemetery itself. I begin my investigations into any cemetery mystery with historical research to glean as much information as possible about the cemetery. I also research the land that was provided for it, along with the person, organization, or society that bequeathed it to the town.

A lot of research is needed to create an accurate picture of any cemetery we investigate—even more so if the cemetery, graveyard, or burial ground is reportedly haunted. Despite the fact that most people believe every cemetery is haunted, this may not necessarily be true. When people encounter unexplained or unusual phenomena, their first response is usually to attach a ghost story to it, and this in turn creates folklore and urban legends that can survive for centuries.

In researching local legends and folklore a good place to start is the local library. Most of the time the librarian can direct you to people who live in the area and can give you additional information about any cemetery, event, or person you are curious about. Nursing homes are also a great place to glean information, especially if you are seeking stories from years past. The staff can usually assist you by introducing you to seniors who are still active and willing to share their stories. And last, but by no means least, visit local diners and restaurants, coffee shops, and local hangouts. There are usually people more than willing to share information. Don't be shy. Once they realize that you are sincere in your quest for information they may actually be eager to assist you.

Gravestones and tombstones are mysterious connections to the past, and often have ghost stories connected to them. However, just because there is a tombstone at the gravesite doesn't necessarily mean that there is also a body there. The person whose name is on the stone may or may not be interred there. It's entirely possible that the gravestone may be no more than a memorial erected by family or friends. The body could have been swept out to sea, lost in a fire, missing in battle, lost due to natural disasters or any number of strange reasons. Of course, these reasons could be even more mysterious than we can imagine and in some cases even sinister. These mysterious cases really fascinate me and I always begin my investigation with the name on the tombstone.

Although names and dates were inscribed on headstones and monuments, they were often inaccurate, cryptic, and in some case just plain bizarre. When people in remote, isolated areas or small towns needed a tombstone it usually had to be ordered from larger towns in surrounding areas. Most of the time the inscription that was to be engraved was sent along with the order for the tombstone. In some cases it took weeks or even months for the stonecutters to finish their design. Most of the engravers were immigrants and it was often hard for them to make out the handwriting on the orders. Sometimes this resulted in names being spelled wrong, dates being misinterpreted, and epitaphs being engraved incorrectly. Nevertheless, the memorial was usually not returned. It was placed at the gravesite with no thought of the problems it would cause future genealogists and historians as well as ghost hunters.

Since those chiseled errors were somewhat commonplace, the dates and names on old tombstones may not be correct and may require additional research to ensure accuracy. Historical societies and local genealogy libraries contain a wealth of information to help validate your findings.

Although tombstone inscriptions, symbols, and artistic designs may be very personal, they eventually become very public displays of memories and intense emotions.

In early America it became necessary for engravers to incorporate symbolism into their art work because many people were not literate. Although they couldn't read or write, they could understand the meaning of angelic messengers, celestial designs, and impressive etchings.

The symbols they choose may express cultural identities, religious affiliations, fraternal organizations, or family ties, as in a family crest. Symbols that are well recognized or regionally specific may mean something entirely different in another part of the country. Of course this also proves true of different eras and periods of time. For this reason alone it is often important to research and understand the history of the cemetery, the area, and the people, as well as the societies they lived in.

Tombstone carvers and engravers often gave artistic meaning to their creations. Because of their creativity their artistic designs may convey different meanings to different people. Unfortunately what they meant to convey by their works of art cannot usually be known to us, especially if years and possibly centuries have passed. Also an engraver's true representation may have been lost to history and folklore; especially as many tombstones were ordered sight unseen.

Always look at the back of a tombstone marker as well as the front for artwork that may reveal additional information. Stonecutters and engravers were very creative and one can never discount artistic vision in designing and engraving markers.

In their creative pursuits they may have been happy, enjoying what they created. Of course they may have also been sad or depressed or perhaps even morose, having lost their muse for one reason or another. Lost in the drudgery of their work, they could have most certainly incorporated these feelings into their work. They may have been of an occult or even mystical mindset and unable to resist including representations of their beliefs in their work. On the other hand, they could have been devoutly religious and intent upon impressing their ideologies of Heaven and Hell on mourners.

You may be able to interpret the meaning of the symbols, designs, and artwork, or you may not. Either way you will probably enjoy the inherent skill and workmanship of the stonecutters and engravers from the past.

A symbol is a sign; an expression to give the impression of something else. As Webster put it; "something concrete that represents or suggests another thing that cannot itself be represented or visualized."

The following is a short list of the most recognized symbols usually found in cemeteries across America. This will help you identify the tombstone art in your area, as well as give you insights into the lives of the deceased.

Acorn: A baby or young child

Anchor: Steadfast, hope

Angel: Flying–rebirth, Trumpeting–call to resurrection,
    Weeping–grief, guardianship, protection
    Bearing a sword–Michael
    Depicted with a trumpet–Gabriel

Arch: Rejoined with partner in Heaven

Arrow: Mortality

Bed: At rest

Bee: Endurance, hard work

Bible: Faith, hope

Bird: Eternal life, resurrection, flight of the soul, the soul

Book: Opened–teacher, closed–minister, book of life

Broken Column: Usually represents the loss of the head of the family

Broken Ring: The family circle has been broken

Buttercup: Cheerfulness

Butterfly: Resurrection

Candle being snuffed: Loss of life

Chain: Broken–loss of a family member

Chalice: Usually represents the Sacraments

Cherub: Innocence

Clock: Passage of time

Coffin: Mortality

Cornucopia: A fruitful life

Cross: An emblem of faith

Crown: The soul's achievement of life after death

Dog: Good master worthy of love, loyalty

Dogwood: Divine sacrifice

Dove: Innocence and/or peace

Drapery: Mourning

Eagle: with FFC-Improved order of Red Men, With FOE-Fraternal Order of Eagles, Double-headed eagles—32nd degree Mason

Fish: Christianity

Flame: Immortality of the spirit

Fleur-de-lis: Passion and love

Fruit: Eternal plenty as in the fruits of life

Garland: Symbol of saintliness

Gates: Gates to Heaven

Grim Reaper: Death personified

Hands: Pointing up–pathway to Heaven, clasped–farewell or the bonds of marriage, praying–asking God for eternal life, hands in general–blessings, with a pen–writing one's name in the book of life

Harp: Praise to God

Heart: Refers to the suffering of Christ, affection for the deceased, joined hearts–marriage

Holly: Usually added as protection from lightning strikes

Honeysuckle: Friendship

Horns: Resurrection

Horse: Courage

Horseshoe: Protection against evil

Hourglass: Time has run out

Iris: Protection

Ivy: Immortality, friendship

KKK: Knights of the Ku Klux Klan

Keys: A learned person, knowledge of the scriptures

Labyrinth: Passage of life

Lamb: Usually marks the grave of a child, innocence

Laurel: A symbol of worldly accomplishments and heroism

Lily: The virgin's flower, innocence and purity

Lion: Courage

Menorah: An emblem of Judaism

Morning glory: Signifies the beginning of life

Oak leaves: Power, authority, victory

Oak Tree: Honor, endurance

Owl: Wisdom, watchfulness

Palm Branch: Victory and rejoicing

Pansy: Remembrance

Peacock: Eternal life, immortality

Poppy: Eternal sleep

Pyramid: Eternity

Rainbow: Fulfillment of the promise of resurrection

Rooster: Awakening, resurrection

Rosebud: Virginity and innocence, wreath of roses—beauty

Rosemary: Remembrance

Roses: Brevity of earthly existence, in full bloom—a full life

Trees: Life everlasting

Scroll: Scriptures

Scythe: An instrument of the harvest, death cuts us down

Shell: Resurrection

Sickle: Reaping of life

Skull, or Skull and Crossed Bones: Death

Spade or shovel: Death

Sphinx: Symbolizes one who is mysterious, guardian

Star of David: Recognized as the international symbol of Judaism

Sun: Renewed life everlasting

Sunburst: With eye–Masonic symbol

Sun dial: Passage of time

Sunflower: Devotion

Sword: Justice and strength

Urn: Remembrance, shattered–old age, draped–mourning

Weeping willow: Perpetual mourning, grief

Wheat sheaf: The divine harvest

Wheel: Cycle of life

Winged face: Effigy of the soul of the deceased

Winged skull: Flight of the soul

Wreath: Victory

AE: An abbreviation for (*Aetatis*) or years of life

BPOE: Benevolent Protection Order of the Elks

CSA: Confederate States Army

DSP: Died without children

DVP: (Latin) died in father's lifetime

DY: Died young

GAR: Grand Army of the Republic

HS: (Latin) here is buried

HIS: (Greek) Christ

IOOF: Independent Order of Odd Fellows

OES: Order of the Eastern Star

Obit Sine Prole: Died without children

Relict: Widow

VFW: Veteran of Foreign Wars

The following information is usually found inscribed on tombstones and monuments, and can be very helpful in shaping the life of anyone you are researching. As for ghosts, this information can also be valuable to investigators and ghost hunters in determining why paranormal phenomena may be connected to a particular gravesite.

1. Names and nicknames of the deceased
2. Maiden names and cultural names
3. Dates of birth and death
4. Marriage and relationships
5. Religious, military, fraternal, and society organizations
6. Lifetime accomplishments
7. Always informative are the biographies that are usually found on elaborate monuments and impressive tombstones
8. Just as interesting and oftentimes humorous are epitaphs

The following things should always be checked whenever possible to add additional insights into any investigation. My personal belief is that one can never do enough research. There is always something to discover. The key is knowing where to look and what questions to ask. The following information is extremely valuable when researching old cemeteries and gravesites:

1. Cemetery records
2. Obituaries

3. Death certificates
4. Funeral home records
5. Autopsy records
6. Coroners' records
7. Newspaper articles
8. Land deeds
9. Historical societies
10. Genealogy departments at local libraries
11. Military service records
12. Fraternal orders
13. Small biographies

Facts do not cease to exist because they are ignored.
—ALDOUS HUXLEY (1894–1963)

Cemetery tombstones and funerary art represent pathways to the past, and if followed with diligence and perseverance will lead the ghost hunter to their ultimate destination: the truth.

SIXTEEN
CEMETERY MYSTERY-RESEARCH FORMS

1. CEMETERY RESEARCH FORM

Date: _____

Full name of deceased: _____

Nickname:_____

Birth date: _____

Death date: _____

Age at death: _____

Husband/wife of: _____

Son/daughter of: _____

Name of cemetery and directions _____

_____

_____

_____

_____

_____

_____

Miscellaneous facts _____

_____

_____

_____

_____

_____

_____

_____

_____

_____

2. COPY THE EPITAPH OR
INSCRIPTION EXACTLY AS YOU SEE IT.

_____

_____

_____

_____

_____

_____

_____

Record any paranormal activity that has been associated
with this tombstone, gravesite, or cemetery.

_____

_____

_____

_____

_____

_____

_____

_____

_____

_____

_____

3. SKETCH THE TOMBSTONE SHAPE
AND ANY MOTIFS OR DECORATIVE CARVINGS.

Describe and / or draw any other interesting or unusual features of this gravesite.

_____

_____

_____

_____

_____

_____

_____

_____

_____

_____

1. GHOST PROFILE

Date: _____

❏ Male   ❏ Female

❏ Benevolent   ❏ Malevolent

Ghost name: _____

Age at death: _____

Life span: _____

Profession: _____

Nationality: _____

Additional information: _____

_____

_____

Cause of death (if known): _____

_____

_____

Manifestation/description: _____

_____

_____

Seen as:

❏ Full apparition

❏ Partial apparition

❏ Shadow ghost

❏ Ecto-mist

❏ Cemetery guardian

❏ Orb

2. RELATED PHENOMENA

❑ Noises

❑ Voices

❑ Smells

❑ Lights

❑ Cold spots

❑ Electrical interference

❑ Seen by others

❑ Captured on film

❑ EVP recorded

❑ Message revealed

Tombstone inscription: _____

_____

_____

_____

Cemetery: _____

_____

_____

_____

Obituary: _____

_____

_____

_____

_____

Newspaper articles _____

_____

_____

_____

_____

3. RUMORS—FOLKLORE—URBAN LEGEND

_____

_____

_____

_____

_____

Notes _____

_____

_____

_____

_____

Final analysis _____

_____

_____

_____

_____

_____

4. CEMETERY MYSTERY: PERSONAL INTERVIEWS

Date: _____

Name: _____

Address: _____

City/state: _____

Phone #: _____

Cell #: _____

Interview: _____

_____

_____

_____

_____

Date: _____

Name: _____

Address: _____

City/state: _____

Phone #: _____

Cell #: _____

Interview: _____

_____

_____

_____

_____

5. CEMETERY MYSTERY

_____

_____

_____

_____

_____

_____

_____

_____

_____

_____

_____

_____

_____

_____

_____

_____

_____

_____

_____

_____

_____

_____

_____

_____

GAZETTEER

Aurora City Cemetery

Aurora, Texas

Aurora is about 25 miles northwest of Fort Worth, Texas. Take US 81/287 to Rhome. Toward Bridgeport take Hwy. 114 and go west 1.5 miles, then south a half-mile on Cemetery Road.

Cedar Grove Cemetery

Dalby Springs, Texas

Located in the Old Dalby Springs Community.

Clara-Glen Pet Cemetery

Kirkland Avenue

Linwood, New Jersey

El Salto Submerged Cemetery

New Mexico

Located 50 miles north of the seaside resort of Mazatlan

Jones Hill Cemetery

Buchanan Road

Texarkana, Texas

Killough Monument

Near Jacksonville, Texas

Go to Jacksonville, Texas, and head north on Hwy. 69. From the intersection of Hwy. 69 and FM 855 go west on 855 until you reach FM 3405. There is a sign that reads Killough Monument and points to the left. Turn left on FM 3405 and go just about .4 miles to FM 3411. Turn right on FM 3411 and go .6 miles until you reach a road with a green gate with a huge boulder on either side. That is actually FM 3431—but there is no sign there. Turn left and proceed through the gate—the monument and cemetery are at the end of road.

L.A. Memorial Pet Cemetery
5068 Old Scandia Lane
Calabasas, California

Marion City Cemetery
Marion, Ohio
Located in the northeast corner of Vernon Heights Blvd. and OH-42

Marshall Ridge Cemetery
780 East Yerby Street
Marshall, Missouri

Meriwether Lewis Monument
Highway 20 Natchez Trace Parkway
Hohenwald, Tennessee

Metairie Cemetery
Pontchartrain Boulevard
New Orleans, Louisiana

Natchez City Cemetery
Natchez, Mississippi
Located on Cemetery Road, on the north side of the city. The cemetery is situated on a bluff overlooking the Mississippi River.

Old Catholic Cemetery
1700 Martin L. King Avenue
Mobile, Alabama

Old Union Cemetery (formerly Dark Corners)
Highway 67 West
Simms, Texas

Red Lick Cemetery
Red Lick Community
Approximately six miles west of Texarkana, Texas. Located in the city of Red Lick, Texas on FM 2148N. Red Lick Cemetery lies to the west and southwest of the Red Lick United Methodist Church.

Rondo Cemetery
Rondo Community
Texarkana, Arkansas
Take US Highway 82E from Texarkana, Arkansas and go for about 4 miles until you get to Arkansas State Road 237, and turn left or north for 1 mile, then at the Methodist church turn right for about 2 miles, and turn left into the gate.

Rose Hill Cemetery
100 South Leila Street
Texarkana, Texas

Rushes Cemetery
Regional Road #5
Wellesley Township, Crosshill
Canada

Salt Lake Cemetery
400 North Avenue
Salt Lake City, Utah

The Salt Lake City Cemetery is located at 400 North and N Street in downtown Salt Lake City, Utah. To find Lilly E. Gray's gravesite: Cemetery Plot Number X-1-169-4E

1. Go to the intersection of 1200 East and 355 North inside the cemetery.
2. Turn your back toward the fence and houses.
3. Look between the 3rd and 4th large pine trees on your left.
4. First stone in her row has the last name "Kidder."
5. The 9th stone in the row is Lilly's enigmatic marker.

Showman's Rest Cemetery/Mt. Olivet Cemetery
Cemetery Road
Hugo, Oklahoma
From town center turn right immediately after Taco Mayo onto 8th street, or take route 70 bypass along the south edge of town and watch for Mt. Olivet Cemetery sign.

St. Louis Cemetery No. 1
3421 Esplanade Avenue
New Orleans, Louisiana
Located 8 blocks from the Mississippi River on the north side of Basin Street and 1 block from the inland border of the French Quarter.

Tobago Island
Caribbean Sea

Violet Cemetery
Highway 39
Konawa, Oklahoma

Waldheim Cemetery
1400 Des Plains Avenue
Forest Park, Illinois

GLOSSARY

Alien: A foreign being different in nature; belonging to another dimension or galaxy; not of our realm of existence.

Angel: Being of light, the medium of spiritual existence; benevolent spiritual being who help and watch over people.

Animate: To fill with breath; to give life to; to quicken; to inspirit; full of spirit.

Anomaly: Something found that has no explainable source; strange unrecognizable shapes appearing in photographs taken at haunted sites and cemeteries.

Apparition: A figure that gives the appearance of being someone the viewer knows to be dead. The disembodied soul or spirit that can be seen visually as a ghost; a spirit that has definite physical features associated with it. Apparitions can be physically seen, recorded, photographed, and may also appear as misty or shadowy figures in varying colors.

Aura: A field of energy surrounding living creatures and entities.

Benevolent spirit: A spirit that is not harmful to humans; a benign spirit that can manifest as physical sightings, smells, and sounds; they often will move objects, turn on or off electrical switches or even gently touch people. Helpful, loving, positive energy.

Bereave: To leave alone, as by death.

Burial: The act or ceremony of burying, especially the act of burying a deceased person; interment.

Burial Grounds: Places where large groups of people were buried before graveyards and cemeteries were established.

Burial Mound: A mound resulting from dirt being piled upon a corpse or corpses.

Burial Vault: More expensive versions of grave liners that are made of copper or steel instead of concrete. They are used to keep the grave from settling. They also allow additional vertical storage space.

Caretaker: One who takes care of the maintenance or security of a cemetery.

Cemetery: A place for burying the dead; Ffrom the Greek *Koimeterion*, meaning a sleeping place; usually located near a church.

Cemetery Sexton: The person in charge of the cemetery and its records; also known as the Superintendent.

Cenotaph: Body not buried where the marker is; an empty grave; a sepulchral monument erected to one who is buried elsewhere.

Churchyard: The grounds surrounding or adjoining a church, often used as a cemetery.

Clairaudience: "Clear Hearing"; a higher faculty of mediumship through which one hears the telepathic impressions of a spirit's temporal voice and speech. Psychic ability to hear sounds or voices that are inaudible to others.

Clairvoyance: "Clear Seeing"; a higher faculty of mediumship through which one sees impressions of a spirit's temporal body and visual memories.

Coffin: A six-sided burial container that is wide at the shoulders and narrow at the feet.

Cold Spot: A definite temperature change in the air or on an object that can't be scientifically explained by drafts. If a spirit wishes to communicate physically or materialize in some way they draw upon the energy of their surroundings and available energy sources, thus creating cold spots.

Columbarium: A vault with niches for urns containing the ashes of the dead. In most cemeteries these niches are encased with front panels of granite or marble that are decorated with a simple name plate.

Coriolis Effect: This is the deflection effect of the earth's rotation on any object in motion which diverts it to the right of velocity in the Northern Hemisphere, and to the left in the Southern Hemisphere.

Corpse Road: A pathway used to carry the deceased to the burial site; these roads were believed to be created along ley lines.

Crematoria: An alternative for families who do not have a grave to mark, but who want a place to focus their mourning and remembrance; carved or cast plaques inside the crematorium which serve this purpose.

Cryptic: Hidden secret occult meaning indicating the use of a code or cipher.

Cryptogram: A piece of writing in secret characters; something written in cipher.

Cryptograph: A cryptogram; a system of secret writing using secret characters.

Cryptology: Occult or enigmatical language.

Cryptonym: A secret name.

Death: The transaction of the soul from material existence to spiritual existence.

Debunk: To show a supposed error.

Deceased: Departed from life; dead.

Desecration: To render unhallowed; to divert from sacred to a profane purpose.

Discarnate: Existing without a physical body; spirits that are free of the body's restrictions.

Disembodied: Functioning energy without physical form.

Disinterred: Removed from a burial plot, or site.

Doppelganger: An apparition that is an exact duplicate of a living person; a projected OBE, either consciously or unconsciously.

Dowsing: The art of using forked sticks or dowsing rods to find graves, water, caves, or oil (also know as radiesthesia).

Effeminate: To make feminine; have feminine qualities; soft, delicate, comforting.

Effigy: A representation or image of something; a sculpted likeness of a person or animal.

Eidoln: An unreal or spectral form; a phantom.

Electromagnetic Field: A field propagated by a combination of electric and magnetic energy which radiates from radio and light waves to gamma and cosmic rays; it is believed that when spirits manifest they create their own energy fields.

EMF: Detector: Handheld scientific instrument that can pick up electronic and magnetic fields over different frequencies; they can read changes and distortions in the natural electromagnetic fields.

Encryption: Encoding information so that only the intended recipient can understand the message by decoding it.

Energy: A intrinsic force through which all entities benevolent, malevolent, or spiritual interact. The essence of all creation; vibrational frequencies of creative power.

Energy Ball: Luminous phenomena typically shaped in a ball form, or irregular patches of light appearing randomly and defying explanation.

Energy Streak: Irregular, zigzag patches of light appearing randomly and defying explanation.

Engraver: One who cuts designs into any hard substance, such as marble, granite, or stone.

Enigma: Anything puzzling or inexplicable, hidden meaning to be discovered.

Entity: A being with an energized life force of some type, including spirits and ghosts.

Epigraph: An inscription on a building or mausoleum.

Epigram: A witty saying or brief poem.

Epitaph: An inscription on a tombstone or monument in memory of the person who is buried.

ESP: The acquisition of information by means beyond the five human senses.

Ethereal Energy: Invisible; delicate and celestial; pertaining to the spiritual atmosphere as opposed to earth; spiritlike.

EVP: Short for electronic voice phenomena. These are voices that are recorded on audio tape when people are not speaking or are not present; these voices often represent a physical manifestation of a spirit attempting to contact the living.

Exhume: To dig up after having been buried; to disinter.

Fairy: A small being or spirit having a graceful human form and superhuman attributes; an elf.

Folklore: The traditional beliefs, customs, and legends of a people that are handed down verbally from generation to generation.

Footstone: A stone marking the foot of a grave.

Freemasonry: An organization that arose from obscure origins in the late sixteenth and early seventeenth centuries. It began as an organization for stonemasons and grew to become a private, elite organization using the stonemason's architectural tools and symbolism in its occult tenets.

Funeral: The ceremony or procession immediately prior to burying or cremating a deceased person.

Ghost: Earthbound, emotional, electrically charged entity; the visual appearance of a spirit or the soul of a deceased person. A disembodied soul or life force.

Ghost Hunter: Someone who researches and documents what they believe to be ghosts or paranormal activity related to ghosts.

Ghost Lore: The practice society has of trying to explain ghostly events by attaching a legend to them.

Ghost Photography: Images of someone you know or someone who is unknown to you showing up in a picture as a full apparition, transparent figure, or just white blurs or mists.

Grave: An excavation in the earth in which a dead body is buried, a cavity into which a deceased person is placed for burial.

Grave Digger: A person who digs the burial place for a deceased person.

Grave Sleeper: A person who sleeps on top of a grave to receive spirit messages.

Graveyard: Resting place for the dead that is usually located in a secluded place and may or may not be near a church.

Hallowed Ground: Ground that has been deemed sacred for burials.

Haunted Ground: A place where a ghost or ghosts frequently return.

Haunting: Refers to a situation where a spirit presence has attached itself to an object, area, or person and has exhibited physical manifestation of their presence.

Headstone: A memorial stone set at the head of a grave.

Heaven: The supreme state of consciousness.

Hell: The lowest state of consciousnesses brought about by choosing to be separate and apart from non-judgmental compassionate love for mankind.

Holy Grail: Any objective of a long difficult quest.

Iconography: The art of symbolic representation using pictures and images of sacred subjects.

Inanimate: Not endowed with life; appearing dead; not breathing in the normal sense of the word.

Infamous: Notorious; disreputable; shocking.

Inscription: Word or words engraved into stone or marble; a mark of respect.

Inter: To bury or place the remains of a dead body into a grave.

Legend: A nonhistorical account, or unverifiable tale, handed down by tradition from earliest times that became popularly accepted as factual.

Ley Lines: Magnetic lines of energy encircling the earth in a grid pattern. Changes in this field are said to influence spirit activity. Invisible lines of natural energy that run horizontally and vertically across the earth. Many sacred, forbidden, haunted sites are located along these lines. Many believe that man is unconsciously drawn to these lines when establishing sacred sites such as burial grounds, stone circles, and cemeteries. It has been suggested that where two lines cross, a portal to other dimensions appears.

Life Force: Pure spiritual energy, the dynamic, animating essence of the soul.

Lycanthropy: A condition where a person believes himself to be a wolf; transformation of a human being into the form of a werewolf.

Malevolent Spirit: A spirit that wishes physical or psychological harm to the living entities around it. Malicious spirits can physically manifest as shoving, biting, scratching, or throwing objects at a person, or they can manifest as partial or full possessions, although these types of spirit activity are very rare.

Manifestation: The appearance of a spirit or ghost taking form. The manner in which ghosts and spirits present themselves.

Mass Grave: A burial cavity where many deceased people are buried together.

Materialization: The sudden appearance of a spirit or object that can be detected with the physical senses.

Mausoleum: A external free standing structure constructed as a building containing the interment space or burial chamber of a deceased person or persons.

Medium: One whose higher psychic faculties are sensitive to telepathic and clairvoyant communication with spirits and ghosts.

MUFON: Mutual UFO Network.

Nature Spirits: Living entities often resembling humans and animals in shape and form but inhabiting a world of their own. They channel etheric energy and are comprised of this same energy. They use their abilities to manipulate energy to assist in the growth of plants and to support nature.

Necropolis: Cemetery or burial place.

Opulence: Endowed with wealth or power.

Orb: a mass of energy in the shape of a ball. There are several classifications depending on size; ghostly apparitions are usually always associated with orb activity; a small ball of light that can be visibly seen or recorded with video or photographical equipment. Orbs can be detected in numerous colors. They will move and often interact with people.

Ossuary: An urn or vault used to hold the bones of the dead.

Pall: The coffin; a covering draped over a coffin, usually of fabric. The origin of the word "Pallbearer" still used today.

Parapsychologist: Derived from the Greek word *para*, meaning "beyond"; literally means "beyond psychology"; the scientific study of paranormal phenomena, the study of a real or supposed phenomenon that appears inexplicable.

Paranormal: Occurrences that take place outside the natural order of things; ghosts, UFOs, ESP; things that are difficult to explain; something that is beyond the range of normal human experience, yet within the realm of the natural.

Phenomena: Something strange; a visible manifestation or appearance of something out of the ordinary; supernatural thing, event, or object.

Portal: Strong energy gateway between the spirit world and our world; access point to other vibrational dimensions.

Potter's Field: Where unknown people are buried.

Psychic: Greek word meaning "of the soul." Phenomena pertaining to higher intuitive faculties. Someone who uses various forms of clairvoyance or empathic feelings to tap into nonphysical realties; someone who is sensitive to the spiritual world.

Quasi: Resembling or alike in certain characteristics or features.

Reality: The state or fact of being real; having actual existence; real as opposed to that which is imagined.

Realm: a sphere of influence; domain; region.

Reincarnation: Belief that the soul returns after death to live in a new body; rebirth of the soul in a new living form.

Reptilian: A race of intelligent, supernatural, highly developed reptile-like humanoids; 6 to 8 feet tall dimensional beings, bipedal, having scaly green skin, large eyes which are usually yellow or gold with a vertical pupil.

Resonate: To vibrate sympathetically in response to vibrations of a particular frequency emitted from another body or entity.

Ritual: Rites or ceremonies of a church or religious body, fraternal, or other affiliated group.

Roadside Memorial: A marker that commemorates a site where a person died suddenly and inexplicably. Unlike a grave tombstone that signifies where the body is laid to rest, the roadside marker defines the last place on earth a person was alive.

Rumor: A current story, report, or statement passing from one person to another without any known authority for truth; hearsay; gossip; an unverifiable story.

Sarcophagi: Stone or iron containers for bodies or coffins, often decorated.

Sacrilege: The stealing or violation of anything sacred.

Sculptor: One who creates artwork that is three dimensional by chiseling and carving; one who creates by molding and forming by hand as with clay.

Sepulchral: Pertaining to burials; to the grave.

Shape-Shifting: A change in the physical form or shape of a person. Physical changes and changes in the general appearance between human form and animal, as well as inanimate objects.

Shaman: A priest or sorcerer among various cultures; one who has the power to deal with and protect against spirits; a medicine man.

Skeptic: Someone who refuses to believe in the existence of ghosts, energy anomalies, and paranormal phenomena; one who doubts, questions, or disagrees with the existence of other dimensions and entities.

Soul: The unifying principal of life; a construct of pure energy; the synergistic whole that unifies and contains one spirit consciousnesses and thought.

Soul effigy: The graphic representation of the soul which is often portrayed in winged form and often exhibits human facial characteristics; a soul effigy is not an angel but rather an image of the soul of the deceased which will be glorified and ascend to heaven.

Spirit: That which is believed to be the principal of consciousness life and the vital source of energy in man. The incorporated part of man regarded as separable from the body at death.

Spirit Profile: Researching the background and history of a ghost or spirit and then determining its consistent patterns as a result of the findings.

Standing Stones: Stones set in vertical positions by man, having magical or religious significance to various cultures.

Statue: A representation of a person or animal carved in stone.

Supernatural: Acts of divine nature; something that occurs or exists through means other than the known forces of nature.

Superstition: Irrational fear of what is unknown; a mysterious belief founded on irrational fears; any ceremony or practice inspired by such a belief, faith in magic, or reverence for charms, omens, visions, and signs.

Taphophile: Lover of tombstones and cemeteries; one who loves to visit cemeteries; often seen taking pictures of gravestones.

Telepathy: Transference of thought; nonverbal thought.

Tignon: A large piece of material or scarf tied around the head to form a kind of turban. Commonly worn by free women of color in early Louisiana Creole societies.

Time Slip: A point in time where the past and present intersect.

UFO: An unidentified flying object; alien spaceship or inter-galactic craft; not of this world.

Undertaker: The person who "undertakes" to make funeral arrangements and to keep the body safe; also known as the funeral director.

Vampire: A reanimated corpse who preys on others.

Vandalism: Destruction of public or private property.

Voodoo: A religion of African origin that is characterized by mysterious rites and practices.

Vortex: A funnel of energy used by ghosts as a conveyance in which to move about easily while at the same time maintaining their energy fields.

Werewolf: a man transformed into a wolf; having the power to assume a wolf's form.

"Nowhere can a secret keep
Always secret dark and deep
Half so well as in the past
Buried deep to last, to last.

—DEAN KOONTZ

BIBLIOGRAPHY

Abbott, Olyne. *Ghosts in the Graveyard*. Plano, TX: Republic of Texas Press, 2001.

Brown, Ron. *Top 100 Unusual Things To See In Ontario*. Boston: Mills Press, 2007.

Coffin, Margaret M. *Death in Early America*. Nashville, TN: Thomas Nelson Publications, 1976.

Garrison, Jim. *The J.F.K. Assassination. A Documentary:* The Garrison Tapes, 1992.

Edwards, Frank. *Strange Worlds*. New York: Citadel Press, 1964.

Hazel, John. *Who's Who in Classical Mythology*. New York: Routledge Publications, 2002.

Historical Society of Oak Park and River Forest. *Nature's Choicest Spot: A Guide to Forest Home and German Waldheim Cemeteries.* 1998.

Klein, Victor C. *New Orleans Ghosts*. New Orleans: Lycanthrope Press, 1962.

Lewis, Chad. *Hidden Headlines of Texas*. Eau Claire, WI: Unexplained Research LLC, 2007.

Marion, John Frances. *Famous and Curious Cemeteries*. New York: Crown Publications, 1977.

Marrs, Jim. *Alien Agenda*. New York: Harper Collins Publications, 1997.

Martinez, Raymond. *Voodoo Queen and Folk Tales Along the Mississippi*. New Orleans: Pelican Publications, 1983.

Meyer, Richard E. *Cemeteries and Graveyards*. Logan, UT: Utah State University Press, 1992.

Mitchell, Clarence Dewey. *Jim, The Wonder Dog*. Point Lookout, MO: School of the Ozarks Press, I. E. Simmermon, 1942.

Morford, Mark. *Classical Mythology*. Oxford University Press, 2009.

Phillips, Ted A. *City of the Silent*. Columbia, SC: University of South Carolina Press, 2005.

Prose, Francine. *Marie Laveau*. Pittston, PA: Berkley Publications, 1977.

Rhoades, Loren. *Death's Garden: Relationships with Cemeteries*. San Francisco: Automatism Press, 1995.

Rhodes, Jewell P. *Voodoo Dreams*. New York: Picador Publications, 1993.

Rule, Leslie. *Coast to Coast Ghosts*. Riverside, NJ: Andrews Mc-Meel Publications, 2001

Schneider, Stuart. *Ghosts in Cemeteries*. Atglen, PA: Schiffer Publications, 2008.

Sloane, David. *Last Great Necessity: Cemeteries in American History*. Baltimore, MD: Johns Hopkins University Press, 1991.

Stott, Annette. *Pioneer Cemeteries: Sculpture Gardens of the Old West*. Lincoln, NE: University of Nebraska Press, 2008.

Tallant, Robert. *Voodoo in New Orleans*. Campbell, CA: Collier Publications, 1962.

Taylor, Troy. *Dead Men Do Tell Tales*. Chicago: Whitechapel Press, 2004.

———. *Haunted Graveyards*. Chicago: Whitechapel Press, 2003.

Warren, Joshua P. *Pet Ghosts*. Pompton Plains, NJ: New Page Books, 2006.

Watkins, Alfred. *The Old Straight Track*. Grand Rapids, MI: Abecus, 1925.

Weil, Tom. *The Cemetery Book: Graveyards, Catacombs, and Other Travel Haunts Around the World.* New York: Hippocrene Books, 1992.

Whitington, Mitchel. *A Ghost In my Suitcase.* Jefferson, TX: Atriad Press, 2005.

———. *Angels of Oakwood.* Jefferson, TX: 23 House Publications, 2006.

———. *Ghosts of East Texas and the Piney Woods.* Jefferson, TX: 23 House Publications, 2005.

ONLINE RESOURCES

www.associatedcontent.com

www.blogarea51.org

www.boozefighters21.com

www.findagrave.com

www.flickr.com

www.forgottenoh.com

www.GhosttoGhosts.com

www.gorvtexas.com

www.graveaddictions.com

www.graveyards.com

www.rense.com

www.roadsideamerica.com

www.theparanormalway.com

www.unmuseum.org/maus

www.waymarking.com

www.weirdnj.com

TO WRITE TO THE AUTHOR

If you wish to contact the author or would like more information about this book, please write to the author in care of Llewellyn Worldwide Ltd. and we will forward your request. Both the author and publisher appreciate hearing from you and learning of your enjoyment of this book and how it has helped you. Llewellyn Worldwide Ltd. cannot guarantee that every letter written to the author can be answered, but all will be forwarded. Please write to:

Melba Goodwyn
℅ Llewellyn Worldwide Ltd.
2143 Wooddale Drive
Woodbury, MN 55125-2989

Please enclose a self-addressed stamped envelope for reply, or $1.00 to cover costs. If outside the U.S.A., enclose an international postal reply coupon.